I0606030
THIS BOOK BELONGS TO:

www.amplifypublishinggroup.com

Via Wonderment: Manifest the Life of Your Dreams

For more information, please contact:
Amplify Publishing, an imprint of Amplify Publishing Group
620 Herndon Parkway, Suite 220
Herndon, VA 20170
info@mascotbooks.com

Library of Congress Control Number: 2025902161

CPSIA Code: PRV0325A

ISBN-13: 979-8-89138-607-5

Printed in the United States

VIA WONDERMENT

MANIFEST THE LIFE OF YOUR DREAMS

by

KAt Gottlieb

To my inner circle—you are the wind beneath my wings, and I appreciate you beyond words.

To those who have gone before—thank you for showing the way.

TABLE OF CONTENTS

Part Two

Preface

Welcome, friend!

Isn't there something so magical about starting a new book? With the promise of adventure transporting us beyond the moment we crack it open, books represent our soul's yearning for more wisdom, wonderment, or pure imagination. It was my inspiration for creating this book.

Throughout its vibrant pages, I hope to introduce you to a whole new world of thoughts by way of the wisdom and wonderment of the law of attraction. To experience the life-changing effects, allow the power of wonderment to open your mind and heart to be curious, amused, enchanted, or even bewildered by it all. While you experience this book, allow yourself to think big, feel deeply, and envision your life in the full spectrum of color! Feel the excitement of new, uncharted parts of your potential coming alive!

With that kind of soulful freedom, I wonder what amazing discoveries await when you open yourself to infinite wisdom and wonderment by way of the law of attraction!

All my best,

Kat

Introduction

My "Why" Behind This Book

My experience with the law of attraction started when I was a young teen. My dad introduced me to a book he was reading about metaphysics. I vividly remember this moment as a dawning of my fascination with topics such as the law of attraction, personal development, and goal achievement. These have been sources of wonderment for me ever since.

I've always been a dreamer and doer. I've always questioned why and experimented with ways to get things done. Perhaps Dad sensed my soulful curiosity, and that's why he encouraged me to read what he called "positive thinking" books. From a young age, I used metaphysics as a motivational and personal development tool. However, my ponderings on the topic weren't "normal" for a Midwestern girl back in the 1980s, when it was more popular to blend in rather than to explore new and different thought processes.

SUPPRESSING YOUR AUTHENTICITY IS LIKE THIS.

I stuffed my interest in the law of attraction under the expected layers of obligations and responsibilities. (Can you relate?) But doing that was like trying to hold a beach ball under water. Eventually, I grew unbearably weary of suppressing my aspirations. So, in my midthirties, I tore apart my life and reconfigured it into something that felt more authentic to me. That may sound exciting, and everything turned out great, but it also was a terrifying, lonely, dark time.

In the ether of metamorphosis, I rediscovered my love for the mysteries of the Universe (capitalized to signify it as a proper noun). I absorbed the wisdom of Dr. Wayne Dyer and Esther Hicks. I fell in love with SARK's (Susan Ariel Rainbow Kennedy's) book *Succulent Wild Woman: Dancing with Your Wonder-full Self*. Don Miguel Ruiz's *The Four Agreements* became my rulebook for living, a book that I've shared with countless others.

Over the next decade, I applied the law of attraction to all areas of my life. As I embraced the wisdom of its principles, my life began to change, and I marveled at the opportunities and helpful people who showed up just when I needed them. The law of attraction became my partner in goal achievement and the key to unlocking my authenticity.

I have many examples of how the law of attraction has enhanced my life in simple and profound ways. By implementing my favorite principle—like attracts like—I found my soulmate by first becoming a vibrational match to the characteristics I desired in a mate. When I met him, I instantly recognized his spirit as a match to mine.

Throughout my career, I've used the law of attraction to inspire and guide my decisions. When I started a bespoke art business, amazing clients found me (instead of the other way around), and my creations delighted customers across the globe. When I decided it was time to sell the business, a buyer walked into my shop looking to acquire it. I cofounded other successful businesses, accomplishing more than I had ever thought possible by keeping my mind and heart (Think/Feel—more on this later) open to receiving all that is meant to be.

Infinite possibilities to explore potential.

What I love about the law of attraction is that it continually expands my horizons. As I accomplish one goal, it ignites the motivation to reach for more. I have learned to trust the Universe, and I deliberately choose to believe in myself. In so doing, the Universe continues to serve me with amazing projects and perfectly suited business partners at just the right time. Delightful events unfold in my life every week. I say this not to brag, but rather to open your mind to the law of attraction's potential to grace your own life. If this can happen for me, it certainly can for you, too!

Because following the principles of the law of attraction has enriched my life to such an extent, I feel compelled to think, write, and speak about their benefits. But to be honest, occasionally my earthly brain (ego) questions my qualifications to author books on this topic. But by honoring my connection to the Universe—whose whispers insistently nudge me to join the conversations of those great thought leaders who helped me create a life of abundance, authenticity, and unlimited potential—I release my inhibitions into the wonderment of it all.

Along the way, I discovered a truth about achievement. Confidence wasn't necessary when I nurtured my sense of wonder. With playful curiosity, I can step out of my comfort zone to explore my potential. Even when I face a challenging new project, like writing this book, I intentionally maintain a harmonious balance of effort and ease because I've learned that's the way to master manifestation.

Every person has been given a unique set of skills and talents (their Authenticity Thumbprint—more on this later) to share with the world. I know my destiny is in simplifying big concepts into easy-to-understand, pragmatic practices and delivering them with joyful creativity. That is, to share the possibilities of the law of attraction with likeminded souls who are seeking their own greatest potential and most authentic life.

Trust your aspirations and your ability to achieve them. It's the Universe calling you to your destiny and greatest life possible.

WHAT I'VE REALIZED
ACHIEVEMENT DOESN'T
REQUIRE CONFIDENCE.
IT'S SIMPLY STAYING IN WONDER
BY ASKING YOURSELF;
"I WONDER IF I COULD DO THAT?"
"I WONDER IF I COULD BE THAT?"
"I WONDER WHAT IT WILL TAKE
TO MAKE IT SO?"
AND THEN, JUST DO THAT.

How to Use This Book

Although there is quite a bit of interest about manifestation and the law of attraction, I identified that there isn't a concise, comprehensive, and relevant book that helps people new to its principles. Many books on this topic overlook key components or, at a minimum, do not provide pragmatic ways to personalize and integrate it into life. This book fulfills that purpose.

There are two parts to this book. The first part describes the historical aspects of the law of attraction and some foundational components of it. It is a primer of sorts to help you understand the who, the what, the where, and most importantly, the why behind its relevance and importance in your life.

The second part of the book goes into greater detail about the seven principles that make up the law of attraction. Each principle is defined, then explained to show why it's important to your manifestation practice. I share examples so that you can begin to understand the life-impacting context of it. I provide suggestions of how to incorporate it into your life and indications that it's working.

To help you intuitively embed the wisdom into your psyche, I offer a variety of thought-provoking opportunities: wonderment moments to pause and ponder life's bigger questions and their personal implications; journal prompts and insightful worksheets to help you explore your thoughts; and simple questions woven throughout the text to personalize your reading experience. By working through these fun exercises, you will begin to internalize each topic and weave its wisdom into your life. I also encourage you to underline, make notes, and flag concepts you want to research further. As you immerse yourself, the magic of the law of attraction will begin to manifest in your life!

THE BEST BOOKS ARE THOSE THAT YOU READ AGAIN AND AGAIN. THROUGHOUT THE YEARS, THEY BECOME DOG-EARED AND HIGHLIGHTED WITH NOTES SCRIBBLED IN THE BORDERS. NOTHING WOULD MAKE ME HAPPIER THAN TO KNOW THIS BOOK GETS LOVED THAT MUCH!

Is it ironic for a motivational how-to book to be set in a gorgeous vacation-like setting?

For many of us, the lush landscape of a dreamy tropical getaway represents an escape from the daily grind, where we can forget about goals and achievements for a while and instead just flow with good vibes.

You see, that's precisely the point!

It's in a relaxed and peaceful vacation-mode mind that we can untether our souls from our everyday concerns. In this easy, breezy headspace, we are free to roam, think freely with flowing emotions, and maybe discover new connections between our thoughts, our feelings, and our most authentic wishes. And when we return to our normal lives, perhaps we will carry back with us new insights to live with an invigorated sense of purpose.

My intention is for you to flow with "wonder-full" vibes as you work through this book!

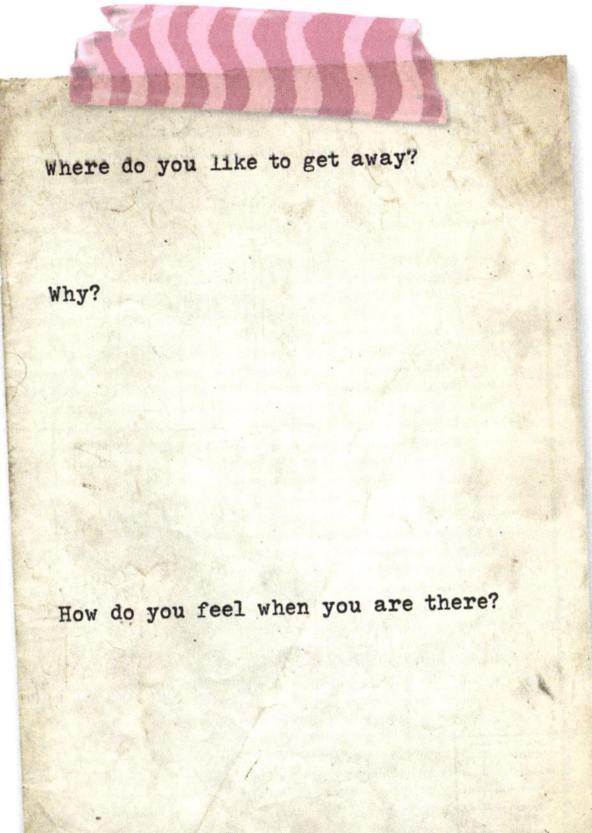

Something to Ponder

When you escape into your imagination, where does your mind travel?

What secret hopes do you find?

How can you find more ways to engage your imagination in daily life?

Write Your Own "Why"

Can you relate to the story that I recounted in the introduction? What are some elements of your own life story that have led to your current situation or interest in the law of attraction?

THE JOURNEY WITHIN

The principles of the law of attraction are full of wisdom and wonderment that are individually enriching as well as powerful as a collective. There are seven principles that we will study in Part Two.

But first, before we can really delve into the riches of them, we need to understand the basic foundation of the law of attraction. Part One, *The Journey Within*, provides historical context as well as "mind, body, soul" concepts that should be understood before the wisdom of the law of attraction can be fully appreciated.

A History of Timeless and Enduring Wisdom

The history of the law of attraction is a curious thing. Its principles cannot be attributed to a single inventor or person. Rather, it's thought to be a collection of principles that various philosophers, scientists, and spiritual leaders have developed and studied throughout the ages. In Eastern philosophy and religion, the principles of attraction have long been studied and applied through concepts such as karma, cause and effect, and the power of intention. Aspects of these principles can be identified in many long-standing religions, although the law of attraction is not attributed to any religious doctrine. Since there isn't one singular originating author behind these principles, there have been many interpretations. Yet the enduring value of the principles of the law of attraction has withstood the test of time, which is a testament to the strength of the law of attraction's wisdom.

The term "law of attraction" is often associated with the New Thought movement of the late nineteenth and early twentieth centuries. The New Thought movement emphasized the power of positive thinking and individuals' ability to create their own reality through their thoughts and beliefs. One of the key figures in this movement was a man named William Walker Atkinson, who wrote many books on the law of attraction, mind power, and related concepts.

In more recent times, the law of attraction has been popularized by authors like Napoleon Hill, Abraham Hicks, Dr. Wayne Dyer, and Sandra Anne Taylor. They have written books based on the principles of attraction, metaphysics, and manifestation. One of the most popular books on the subject, *The Secret* by Rhonda Byrne, published in 2006 and turned into a documentary, raised contemporary awareness of the law of attraction. And since then, the topic has reached even more people by way of social media. As the law of attraction reaches mass appeal, content creators and promoters of programs and products are choosing to market it as a formula to "get rich quick" or "find a soulmate fast." This oversimplification of the principles overshadows the deeply meaningful and fulfilling aspects of the law of attraction. The real value of it is to help individuals become aware of their mindset by intentionally choosing their thoughts and actions to create a better life experience.

The law of attraction can guide our personal values when we realize we are connected to the collective flow of the Universe. We can access infinite wisdom by aligning our thoughts and emotions to a desired state of being. As we practice the law of attraction more, our potential may surpass our wildest aspirations. That is the wonderful magic of it all!

Always present and accessible to all.

"The Universe" is a term deeply connected to the law of attraction. Not to be confused with its scientific reference to the "observable universe" of stars, galaxies, and endless space above the sky, the Universe, as used within this context, is a name for the generalized concept of life force or source energy, much like terms such as God or creator.

The Universe is regarded as a vast and interconnected system that includes all matter and energy and the space and time in which everything exists. In addition, it is the driving force behind reality as we know it—the tangible things that we see, hear, taste, touch, and smell, as well as intangible things like intentions, thoughts, and emotions. Within the Universe, we are all connected, and it responds to our thoughts and feelings, always "listening" and "responding" to the vibrations that we send out via our thoughts and corresponding emotions.

What makes the law of attraction so different from many religious practices is that the Universe is a benign, benevolent power. It does not judge, suppress, or punish. Instead, think of the Universe as a mirror that is simply reflecting to us and supplying us with opportunities that match what we put out into the world. Because the law of attraction is reliable and consistent for everyone without societal or religious doctrine, it impacts everyone the same, and anyone can put it to use to create the life experiences they wish to have.

Impartial, impersonal, yet precise and exact.

The causes and effects of the law of attraction are always at work and present, whether we know it or not. It is impartial and impersonal, yet precise and exact. It affects our lives in every moment, undoubtedly the most dramatic yet understated influence on the quality of our reality.

To provide a simplified comparison, the law of attraction acts in a similar manner to gravity by governing how we interact with the physical world. Like gravity, the law of attraction is an invisible force that can have a powerful impact. While gravity keeps us rooted to the ground and affects how objects interact in the physical world, the law of attraction affects our thoughts, feelings, and actions, shaping our physical reality in powerful and meaningful ways.

However, even as the law of attraction is constantly and naturally affecting our lives, it differs from gravity in that it's up to individuals to use it with intention given their own unique set of circumstances. It is always malleable. At any given moment, you can choose a different energy to focus on, instantly changing your awareness of reality.

Proving the existence of the law of attraction.

Although science and metaphysical concepts tend to have a tenuous relationship, quantum physics has begun to make exciting discoveries about the mysteries of energy and matter, and many of its theories align with the wisdom of the law of attraction. Neuroscience also continues to delve deeper into the interconnectedness of the physical functions of the body and the nonphysical processes of the brain and our perceptions of reality and spirituality. As these and other interdisciplinary sciences explore energy, vibration, and their effect on matter and consciousness as a fundamental process of nature, they draw ever closer to the commingling of scientific wisdom and the wonderment of the law of attraction.

We are amid an exciting time in human evolution as we uncover ever more details about consciousness, reality as we know it, and the potential of the human mind. The law of attraction is a fascinating way to begin to explore your own potential!

Pause for a moment to digest the details. What part of the law of attraction fascinates you the most?

What conflicts with what you were taught to believe?

What part (or parts) do you want to research in greater depth?

FREEDOM

Circle the words that feel like freedom to you.

Independence Attention
Clarity Focus
Thoughtful Choice Free
Possibilities Joy
Interpretation Opportunity
Relax Options Meaningful
Release Redemption
Truth Infinity Excite
Expansion Growth
Power Adventure
Safe
Bold Creative Authentic
Confidence Ease Peace
Self-determination
Achievement Liberty Deliverance
Play Autonomy
Flexibility Success

Add some of your own words:

____

____

____

Freedom of Interpretation

Unlike other doctrines, practicing the law of attraction comes with no requirements or restrictions. You are free to apply the principles within your life as you desire. Although the powers of the law of attraction are always at play in your life (and everyone's lives equally), it is up to you to decide if you want to put them to use with intention. The Universe doesn't require you to follow its principles, nor does it punish you if you don't; the principles continue to affect you the same. The opportunity to apply the wisdom of the law of attraction is completely at your discretion.

Interpretation, and the introspection that precedes it, is a big part of the law of attraction. As you decide how to think and feel about the circumstances of your reality, you are choosing the power of your vibrations and, consequently, the direction of your life situations. As you study the wisdom of the law of attraction, you can begin to harness it for your betterment. That is the power at your fingertips!

I find it fascinating that I can study the law of attraction throughout my life, and as my circumstances change, so does my interpretation of the principles. With every year, as I earn more wisdom, I see new ways to apply what I've learned. New opportunities and viewpoints provide endlessly expanding horizons of my psyche and reality.

The law of attraction is wisdom that we can freely apply without exception to every part of life.

The Way of Communication with the Universe

Energy is a metaphysical concept that suggests we can attract positive or negative experiences into our lives based on the energy that we put out into the Universe, emitted through our vibrations.

In physics, energy is defined as the ability to do work, which can be measured and quantified through various scientific methods. Energy can take many different forms. When you look at the microscopic particles of nature, you realize everything is made up of energy. The law of attraction also states that we are all connected by means of energy. Because everything in the scientific definition of the universe is made of energy, we realize that we are not separate from the metaphysical Universe (a.k.a., life force, source energy).

We, along with everything in this world, are an inseparable, complex, and interconnected flow of energy that is the Universe.

Frequency, within the context of the law of attraction, refers to the energetic vibration that our thoughts, feelings, and actions emit. According to this principle, every thought, feeling, and action has a unique frequency, and we attract matching frequencies of people, things, and circumstances.

Like a radio signal, our frequency can be deliberately "tuned" to connect with desired frequencies. We can attract positive experiences, people, and circumstances into our lives by aligning our thoughts and feelings with what we want. According to this principle, if we focus on positive thoughts and feelings, we will attract positive experiences and outcomes into our lives. On the other hand, if we focus on negative thoughts and feelings, we will attract negative experiences and outcomes. The cumulative result of our habitual thought processes and corresponding emotional reactions becomes, in essence, a self-fulfilling prophecy. What you think about and how you feel about it determines what you perceive in your reality.

The *now* dynamic.

The Universe runs on a simple formula: there is no past or future. The only reality that has relevance is this exact moment, then it's gone and only a figment of our memory, and on to the next moment.

Here is the soulful manifestation wisdom of the now dynamic: carrying your past is a choice, unnecessary or irrelevant to the principles of the law of attraction. Every memory that you cling to, every regret or shame that you harbor, brings its residual energy back into your body when you recall it. Your mind doesn't know that it's past, as it triggers emotions, causing you to relive it all again.

Worrying about the future is also a choice. Since the only power we have is in this moment, fretting about the future distracts us from our power center, the now. But, once again, our minds don't know the difference between reality and thoughts, so when we make up bad things in our minds, we create negative emotions that generate low frequencies via our thoughts. These frequencies send out vibrations that connect to matching negative energies.

Most often, what we worry about never happens, but those simple negative emotional triggers will impede our manifestation process.

ALIGNMENT

OCCURS WHEN WE ARE IN HARMONY
WITH THE ENERGY OF THE UNIVERSE.
WE ATTRACT EXPERIENCES, PEOPLE, AND
CIRCUMSTANCES THAT MATCH OUR ENERGY.
WE CAN IMPROVE AND REFINE OUR ALIGNMENT
WITH PRACTICE, AND THEREFORE,
MANIFEST WITH ACCURACY.

Think/Feel—the Way of Manifestation

There is a powerful relationship between our thoughts and our corresponding emotional processing of those thoughts. I call it Think/Feel. When these two elements—our thoughts and connected feelings—are intentionally aligned and deliberately focused, our goals manifest accurately and swiftly.

Here's how it works: Our Think/Feel sends a strong vibration into the Universe (like a radio signal) that connects with similar frequencies. It bears repeating to remember that "like attracts like"—positive to positive, negative to negative.

Whatever you consistently focus on and emotionally resonate with will be drawn into your reality.

Extreme transparency of manifestation.

The law of attraction doesn't lie, and you can't fool it either. It is the ultimate truth! Because of the incredibly consistent transparency of its principles, what manifests in your life is directly related to your thoughts and emotions. Because of this extreme authenticity of the law of attraction, what manifests is not what we wish for, but what we believe. Our life experiences are dependent on what we habitually think about and emotionally resonate with.

Yet most of us are not fully aware of how our thoughts and emotions impact our lives. Every decision we make and belief we have originates within ourselves, whether we are conscious of it or not. Then, when we attach meaning by way of our emotions, manifestation begins. In essence, we choose what we manifest by what we think about, what we believe (especially about ourselves), and what actions we take because of our inner processing.

Most people are prisoners of their minds and emotions simply because they aren't aware that much of their Think/Feel is a result of habits. They get in a rut thinking and reacting a certain way, without much awareness of the important connection to manifestation. However, to control what you manifest, you must learn how to overcome negative habits and focus your thoughts and emotions in better, more desirable directions. This is the power of proactivity and choice that is the foundation of the law of attraction.

Your Think/Feel is the single most powerful tool to dynamically change the course of your life. And the good news is that you are completely in charge of it.

No one else can determine your Think/Feel.

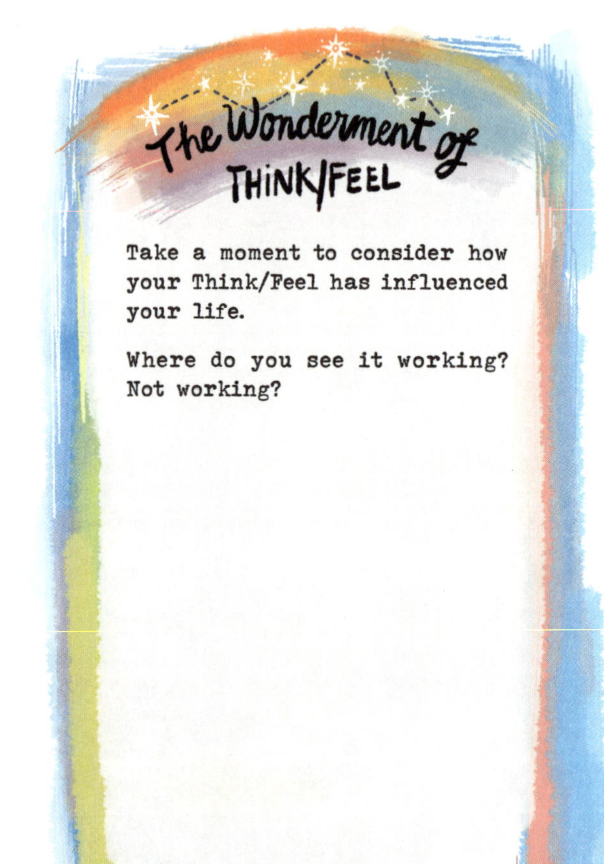

THINK/FEEL

YOU ATTRACT ENERGY AND ALL LIFE EXPERIENCES BY THE VIBRATION YOU EMIT THROUGH THE COMBINATION OF YOUR THOUGHTS AND CORRESPONDING EMOTIONS.

YOUR VIBRATION CONNECTS WITH MATCHING (SIMILAR) VIBRATIONS AT YOUR POINT OF MANIFESTATION.

Defining Your Think/Feel

Imagine your best life experience. Describe it here. Use words that are as descriptive as possible.

Now, circle the words that resonate the strongest. Write those words inside the heart shape on the next page, and color the artwork around it.

MY LIFE IS FILLED WITH

TAME YOUR BRAIN
CREATE SPACE IN YOUR PSYCHE SO THE UNIVERSE CAN SPEAK TO YOUR SOUL.

THIS LITTLE REALIZATION HELPED SHAPE MY THINK/FEEL MORE THAN ANYTHING ELSE THAT I HAVE EVER LEARNED!

Tame Your Brain to Master Manifestation

If you can capture this one bit of wisdom, your life will change forever: Your thoughts *do not* have to define or dominate your life experience. You can learn how to pick and choose your thoughts and emotions as you want instead of letting them run out of control. You can do this by understanding the very simple concept of your Think/Feel.

Not every thought is worthy of your attention! Thoughts are simply passing noise in our psyche. It is entirely normal to have a wide spectrum of thoughts, positive to negative. (Even masters of manifestation still possess occasional less-than-desirable thoughts.) But, according to the law of attraction, thoughts are not important until we begin to resonate with them via our emotions. Then, they create our Think/Feel, the fuel that ignites manifestation.

As we become aware of this key concept, we can begin to deliberately manage our Think/Feel in the direction of our preferred state of mind. It is possible by first creating a sense of detachment from our mental processes. Doing so can help us develop greater self-awareness, cultivate a more positive and empowered mindset, and reduce the impact of negative or intrusive thoughts on our well-being and manifestation power.

You can improve your Think/Feel by training your brain to focus on the things you wish to manifest. Just like anything else, the more you practice it, the better you get. So, allow yourself plenty of time and grace as you begin the life-changing practice of intentionally nurturing your Think/Feel. Instead of trying to suppress a thought, which is nearly impossible to do, I recommend that you shift your focus to a better, more agreeable, or productive thought. Its emotional resonance improves as the thought lifts into a more positive state. The goal is simply to find a way to "feed" the good thoughts and "starve" the others. The law of attraction will take care of the rest!

This works even when we need to process difficult decisions. Sometimes we assume that once we learn the way of the law of attraction, we will never have tough or complex challenges; however, no life is without them, and no mind is pure positivity. Even the best life has its demanding moments. But as you master manifestation, you will learn how to minimize the negative to expand the positive by merely shifting your focus. For example, instead of obsessing over a problem, focus your thoughts on problem solving. Do you see how that tiny shift in mindset dramatically changes the focus of your thoughts and feels better too? Pause and *feel* the difference!

As you begin to experience the way of the law of attraction, you will realize how important your Think/Feel is to improving your life experience. The more you intentionally work with it to reap the benefits, the less likely you will be to allow your mind or emotions to dwell in negativity, whether that negativity comes from self-imposed thoughts or the opinions of people around you. Because of the consistent mirror-like nature of the law of attraction, you can gauge the effectiveness of your Think/Feel by how your dreams and goals manifest and, most importantly, how you appreciate your life journey.

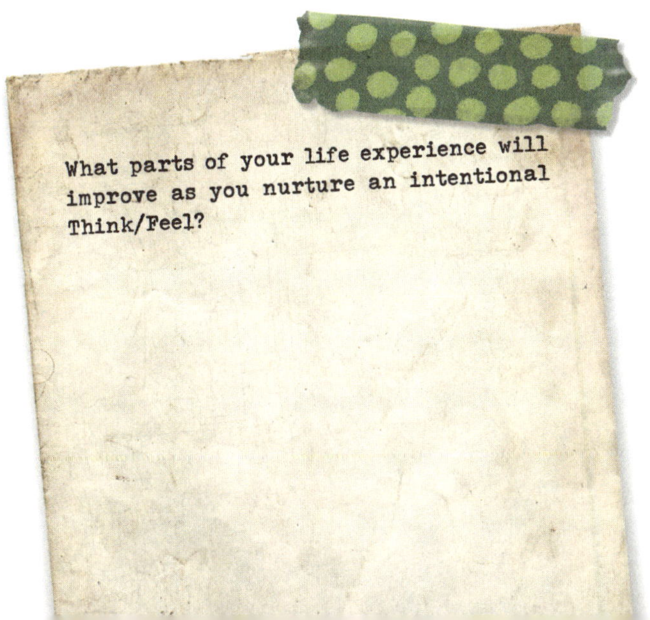

How to Filter Your Think/Feel

You are in charge!

It is empowering to know that you can filter your thoughts to manifest with accuracy.

Instead of allowing every thought to carry equal weight of your attention, you can select those that support your greater good. Since our minds can only focus on one thought at a time, we can empower this principle to filter our Think/Feel. As we focus on our preferred way of thinking, the other thoughts cannot take up emotional or intellectual space. We no longer send vibrations in those directions; therefore, less desirable thoughts simply dissipate without affecting our points of manifestation.

As you identify your preferred thoughts, you can focus on them, enjoying the feeling of them and appreciating how they will bring more goodness into your world. Imagine more beneficial thoughts, and in this process, negative thoughts slip away. It's really that easy and intuitive!

At first, it takes practice to become aware of your thoughts and then to focus on the best option. But as you practice, you will get better at it. And the better you get at focusing your Think/Feel, the more masterfully you will manifest what you desire.

Water what you want to grow.

When you become aware of your thoughts and connected emotions, ask yourself, "Do I want to experience these more or less?"

If you are resonating in a negative or not preferred topic, do not feel bad about it; congratulate yourself! You see, when you become aware of your Think/Feel, you can begin to direct it with intention! When you catch yourself mulling about in negativity, ask yourself, "What would be a preferred (productive, pleasant, etc.) Think/Feel?" And go there instead.

Imagine how your thoughts can help you make positive changes. How can your emotions support your efforts?

Can you identify or describe your preferred Think/Feel?

DECIDE WHICH ONES TO KEEP

BASED ON WHAT YOU WANT TO MANIFEST,

AND LET THE REST GO.

TO BEGIN FILTERING YOUR THOUGHTS, SPEND PLENTY OF TIME VISUALIZING WITH EXTREME CLARITY WHAT YOU WANT IN YOUR FUTURE. THEN, YOU WILL KNOW WHETHER THE THOUGHTS SUPPORT OR DETRACT FROM YOUR DESIRED REALITY.

I Want More!

List ten things that you want more of.

Describe how those things will make you feel. Use language that is as descriptive as possible. Feel the words that you use.

1. __________
2. __________
3. __________
4. __________
5. __________
6. __________
7. __________
8. __________
9. __________
10. __________

Now, identify proof—any indication, no matter how small or faint—of that reality already manifesting in your life. Even tiny hints of what you want, the Universe is already trying to deliver. Express gratitude for every bit of manifestation to expand your heart and mind to receive more.

Continue to look for evidence every day.

How do you understand or emotionally process this quote?

Can you identify instances when your beliefs restricted or actualized your potential?

The Alchemy of Wisdom and Wonderment

There's a very practical application of the principles of the law of attraction that provides great wisdom: cause-and-effect guidelines that need to be studied and practiced. But there is an even more powerful and profound aspect critical to success that is often overlooked.

The mystery and magic of the Universe are opened with emotions that vibrate high and wide. Wonderment is such an emotion. It is the gateway to creativity, innovation, and invention. Wonderment, and the yearning to understand and explore, is a core impulse of the human psyche.

Wonderment is a complex emotion that contains elements of surprise, contemplation, joy, and, most importantly, a heightened state of consciousness where energetic frequency opens to the Universe's infinite wisdom. We empower the law of attraction when we value an equal balance of wisdom and wonderment to be open to its inspiration, nudges, and direction by way of our instincts, feelings, and emotions. When we are in touch with the Universe, we make better, more aligned decisions, connect with people and events with similar vibrations, and in general, feel life unfolding to our liking. Working in concert with the Universe, we also begin to experience wonderful coincidences, amazing synchronicities, and outright miracles. Our sense of wonderment is the magical conduit for all of this.

Yet wisdom is valued more by society. We're taught wisdom; at least twelve years of our young lives are spent sitting at a desk, learning it as the path to our future. We are told that it is more important than our youthful, wild sense of wonder. It's no wonder that many of us reach adulthood feeling part of us is missing. What's lost—or, I should say, educated out of us—is our sense of wonderment, our naive fascination, and our trust in the unknown. We become constricted with "facts," what we "know," and doubt the existence of anything that cannot be proven according to contemporary "experts."

The problem so many people have when they begin to study the law of attraction and the ways of manifestation is that they are accustomed to being good students via the educational system. What goes missing is the component of an open and trusting wonderment mindset. People try to make manifestation work by hustling and working hard, thinking that the key to success is what we were taught in school, but it's not the same. As a result, our emotional set point does not align with our efforts.

For example, we may say we want something, but inside, we worry or doubt it will happen. We overthink or create negative, anxious, or uncertain vibrations that are incongruent to the manifestation of our goals and desires.

For manifestation to work, we need to open our energy to the powers of the Universe; listening to, allowing, and flowing to its rhythms and timing. Then the Universe can do its thing: bring our authentic wishes and desires to us by way of coincidences, inspiration, or intuition. When we have authentic trust in the process, there is no end to the possibilities.

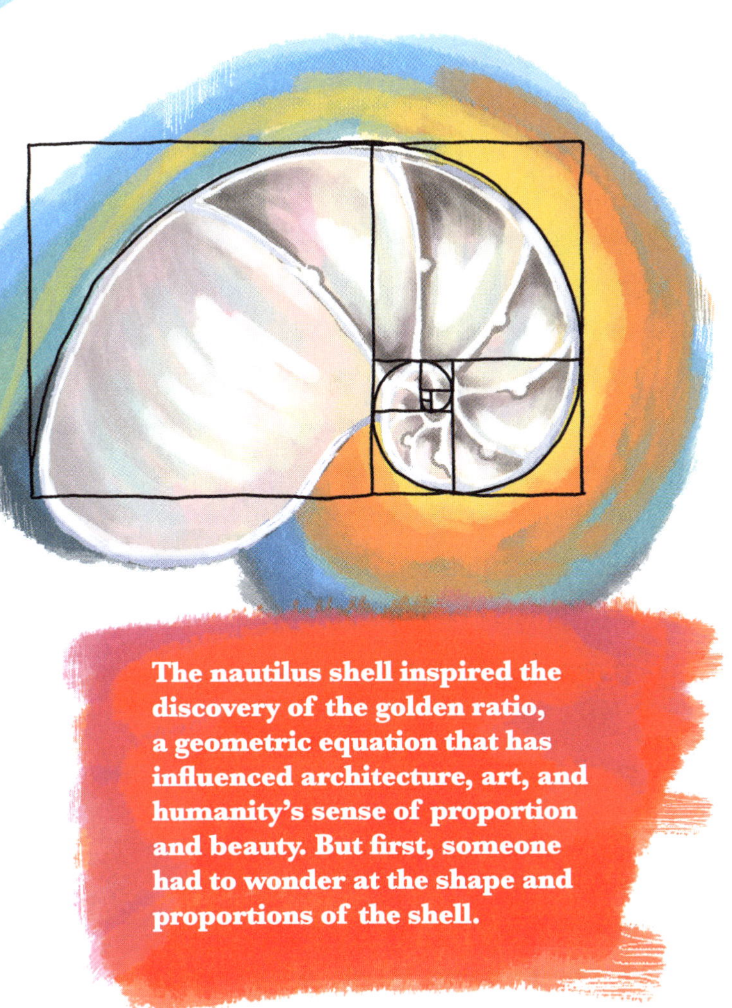

The nautilus shell inspired the discovery of the golden ratio, a geometric equation that has influenced architecture, art, and humanity's sense of proportion and beauty. But first, someone had to wonder at the shape and proportions of the shell.

Opening up your soul to a sense of wonderment allows manifestation to flow. When you authentically embrace the teachings of the law of attraction, you will reenergize your senses in the mystical but harmonic balance between wisdom and wonderment. You will find a new world of vivid beauty and meaningful intensity. With wonder in your eyes, you will find every detail of life fascinating and revel in your place within it. You will begin to witness miracles happening all around you and see them blessing your life already.

As you continue to watch for goodness, because of the principles of the law of attraction, you will attract more of the same into your reality.

And the good news is that you can learn to develop and nurture the key emotional component of wonderment, which this book focuses on. You can improve your Think/Feel accuracy by following the practices, exercises, and worksheets in this book. And this will work intuitively, meaning that you will naturally begin to shift your emotional set point as you focus on the right things. You don't have to overthink, work harder, or force yourself to change. It should be a natural occurrence that feels better to you—lightening your mood with more meaningful, calming emotions so you are encouraged to do it more often.

Again, according to the law of attraction, what you focus on expands in your reality; you continue to feel success, and as a result, it draws more to you. And in that process, you will begin to manifest more strongly, more consistently, and much more predictably.

The Wonderment of WONDERMENT

Take a moment to feel wonderment (you can pick a topic that elicits a sense of awe, imagination, or fascination). Enjoy the opening of your soul as it expands into the Universe.

Where could you benefit from allowing more wonderment into your life?

How to Re-Engage Your Wonderment
PONDER THE EXISTENCE OF LIFE IN ANOTHER GALAXY
MARVEL AT THE MIRACLE OF BIRTH

FIND A QUIET SPOT AND WATCH THE WORLD UNDERFOOT
ASK AN ELDER TO SHARE THEIR LIFE STORY

WISDOM BEGINS IN WONDER
~SOCRATES~

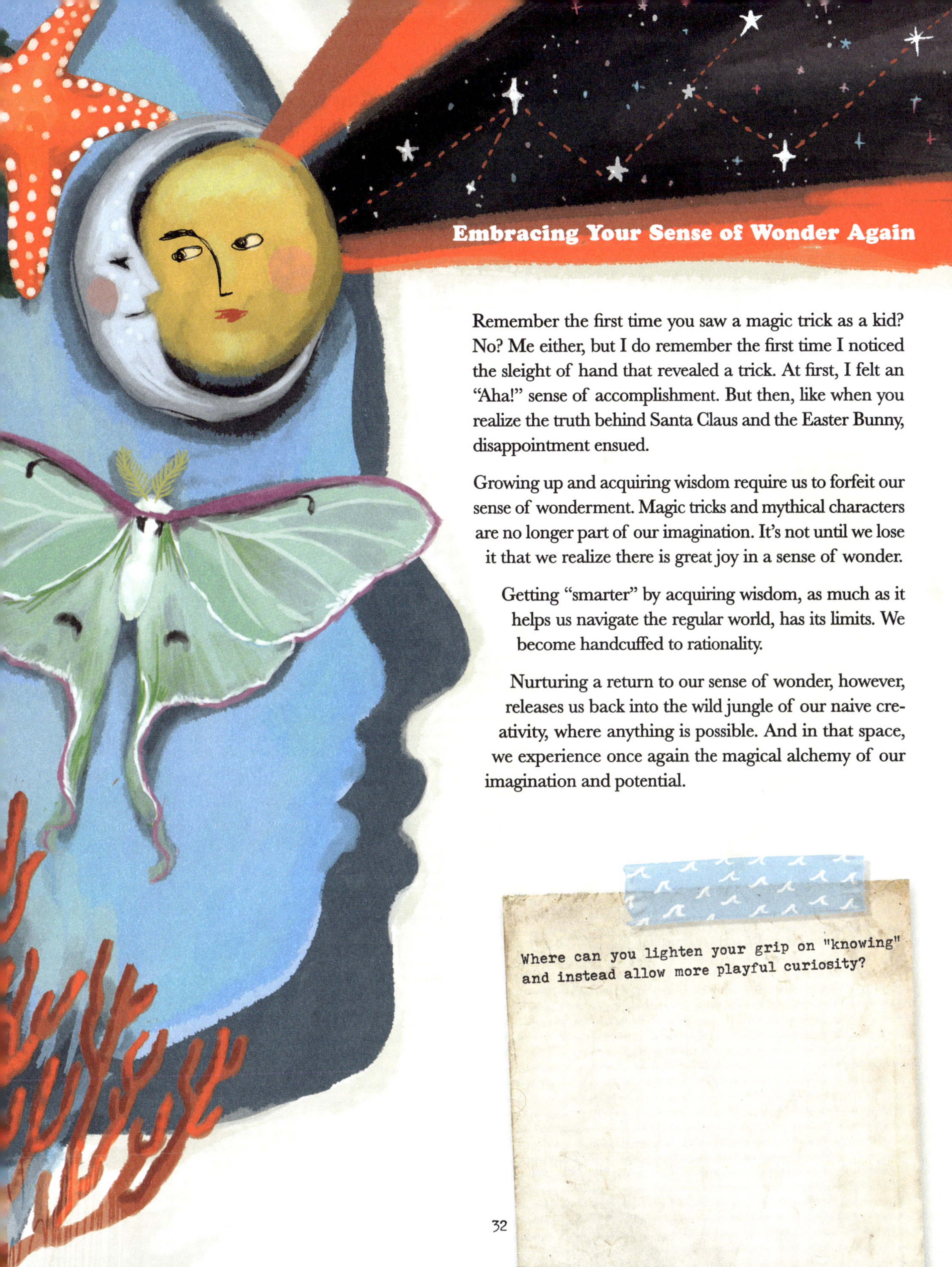

Embracing Your Sense of Wonder Again

Remember the first time you saw a magic trick as a kid? No? Me either, but I do remember the first time I noticed the sleight of hand that revealed a trick. At first, I felt an "Aha!" sense of accomplishment. But then, like when you realize the truth behind Santa Claus and the Easter Bunny, disappointment ensued.

Growing up and acquiring wisdom require us to forfeit our sense of wonderment. Magic tricks and mythical characters are no longer part of our imagination. It's not until we lose it that we realize there is great joy in a sense of wonder.

Getting "smarter" by acquiring wisdom, as much as it helps us navigate the regular world, has its limits. We become handcuffed to rationality.

Nurturing a return to our sense of wonder, however, releases us back into the wild jungle of our naive creativity, where anything is possible. And in that space, we experience once again the magical alchemy of our imagination and potential.

Where can you lighten your grip on "knowing" and instead allow more playful curiosity?

Take a Recess from Stress to Reconnect with Your Childhood Sense of Wonder

What were your favorite playtime or recess activities? How can you reintroduce them into your life? Draw a picture of yourself enjoying this activity.

GIVE YOURSELF UNSTRUCTURED TIME TO PLAY EVERY DAY. EVEN FIVE MINUTES WILL BE RECUPERATIVE TO YOUR SOUL.

Heal Your Inner Child

Write a letter to your younger self. Pick a time in your past when you would like to send yourself healing comfort or encouragement. Here are some prompts to get you started:

- Consider what you were told about yourself when you were young. How did it make you feel then, and how does it make you feel now?
- Remind your younger self of strengths or talents that may have been overlooked by others, or by yourself.
- Encourage your inner child to release worry, fear, or other undesired impediments to your greatest good.
- Promise to heal the areas of your memory that inhibit your self-esteem.

After you complete this letter, decide what you would like to do with it. Will keeping it empower or disempower you? If you keep it, will you store or display it?

Instead of keeping it, perhaps you can burn it and watch the smoke and ash drift off. Or, you can put it in a bottle and send it out to sea.

Dear Younger Me,

I Love You Unconditionally
and forever,

Wonderment Nurtures Intuition

Manifestation is strongest when you are open to the ethereal, nonphysical, but very real guidance of the Universe. This line of communication is often referred to as intuition or gut instinct. It is your inner knowing when something "feels right" or warning when something is amiss. Every highly successful person I know relies on their intuition in some fashion. They have mastered the ability to discern the path to achievement by trusting their instincts. There are other words to describe this inner knowing, but they all center on the same power to visualize solutions with clarity or sense or predict future events.

There is a gateway to higher consciousness and connection to the Universe.

It's more than just a strong imagination or luck; it is a connection to something beyond our human senses. Or more precisely, it's an amalgamation of our senses, registering nuances in our environment and converging with the Universe, which informs us of how to react to the situation at hand.

Many of us hinder our intuition by relying too heavily on intellect or falling prey to our emotions. But, as we realize that the Universe speaks from a place of benevolence, we learn to trust what it tells us. When we go beyond our human senses, we access our connection to divine wisdom and align our manifestation vibrations to benefit our situation. Learning to master the law of attraction includes connecting to this vital source of guidance and truth.

Nurturing our sense of wonderment taps into that place beyond our earthly limits where we can benefit from this source of power. As a technique, reawakening our playful sense of wonderment intuitively leads us to this mystical, magical state.

Manifestation occurs swiftly and accurately.

When your sense of intuition is strong, you can manifest with amazing speed and accuracy. Your inner knowing works like an internal GPS, showing you the way to make things happen or alerting you to predict and navigate obstacles. Your Think/Feel is refined, and as a result, your confidence grows in your ability to make good decisions, intrinsically know what's right, and take the chances that bring about success. What others attribute to luck you know to be your connection to the higher powers of the Universe.

YOUR CONNECTION TO THE UNIVERSE IS A KNOWING THAT MANY PEOPLE CALL INSPIRATION, INSTINCT, INTUITION, PREMONITION, LUCK, DREAM, CALLING, CONSCIOUSNESS, ET CETERA.

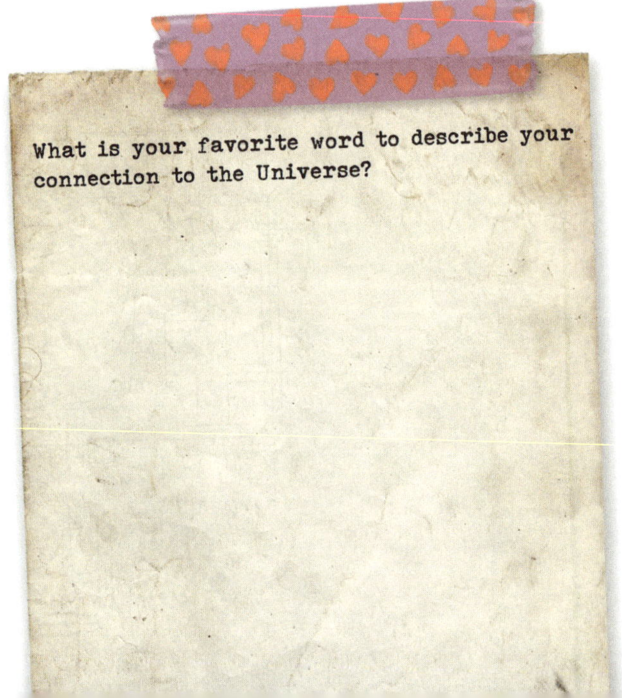

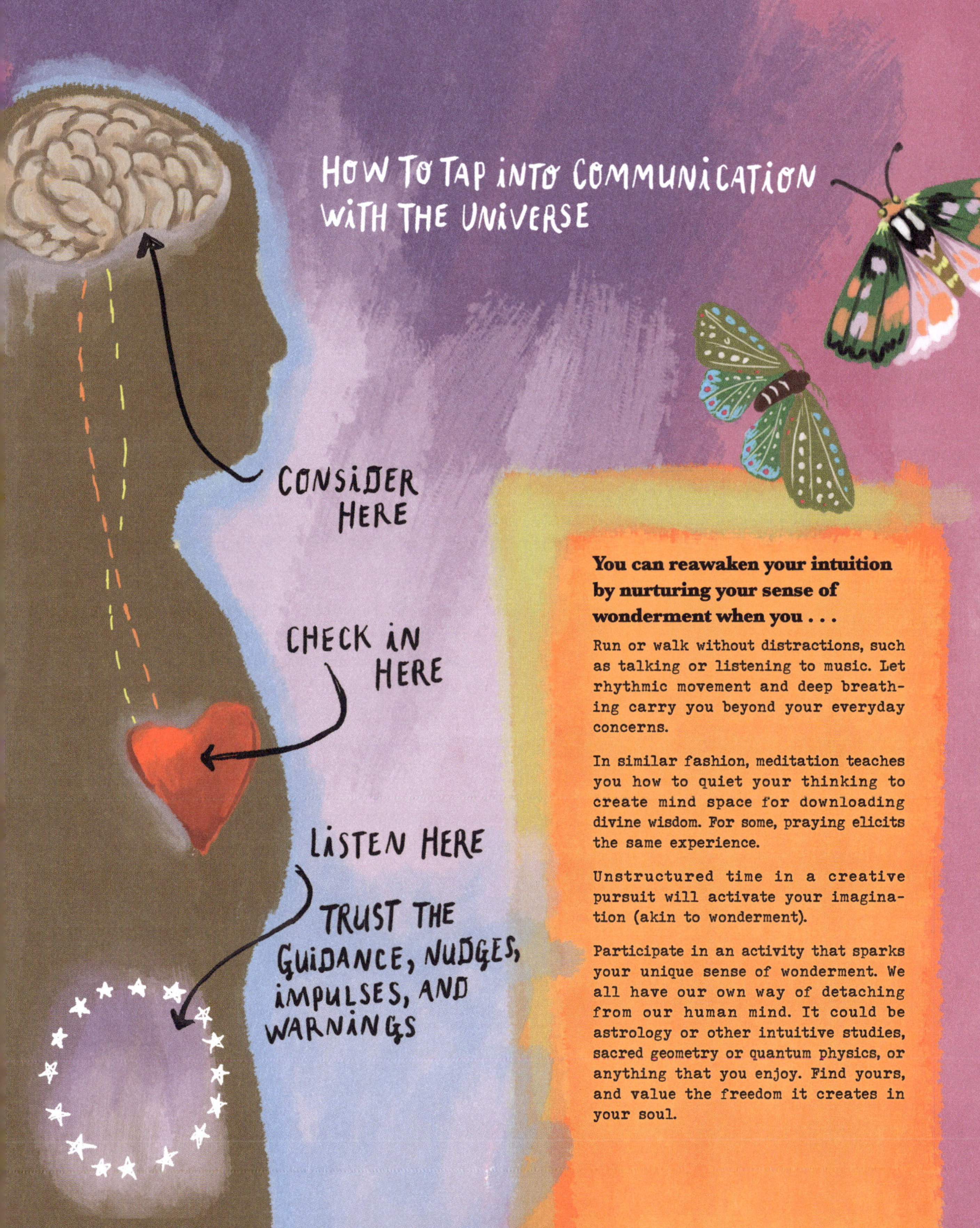

You can reawaken your intuition by nurturing your sense of wonderment when you . . .

Run or walk without distractions, such as talking or listening to music. Let rhythmic movement and deep breathing carry you beyond your everyday concerns.

In similar fashion, meditation teaches you how to quiet your thinking to create mind space for downloading divine wisdom. For some, praying elicits the same experience.

Unstructured time in a creative pursuit will activate your imagination (akin to wonderment).

Participate in an activity that sparks your unique sense of wonderment. We all have our own way of detaching from our human mind. It could be astrology or other intuitive studies, sacred geometry or quantum physics, or anything that you enjoy. Find yours, and value the freedom it creates in your soul.

Crafting Your Reality with Intention

Goal achievement is a natural extension of the law of attraction. We manifest our desires by focusing our thoughts and energy on them. Likewise, by setting specific goals and visualizing their accomplishment, we can align our thoughts, emotions, and actions with our desired outcomes, which can increase the likelihood of their manifestation. By combining the law of attraction with pragmatic goal-setting techniques, we can create a powerful mind, body, and soul synergy in the direction of our dreams. It helps us stay motivated, focused, and aligned with our goals, thereby propelling us forward.

As you improve your understanding of the principles of the law of attraction, goal achievement becomes a natural interest. With its power working with your efforts, you can accomplish anything you desire. Achieving goals becomes a fun game of sorts that is thrilling and joyful to play.

Instead of resigning yourself to reacting to what life throws at you, use the knowledge and tools of the law of attraction to steer your mind, and use the flow of the Universe to propel you toward the energy that you desire.

The real goal is becoming the best version of yourself.

Personal development is at the core of the law of attraction because, as exciting as chasing goals and achieving the objects of your desires feel, the real value of the principles is how they shape your inner concept of yourself. Regardless of your goals, the principles provide guidance on how to be the best version of yourself. That alone makes studying them worthwhile. When you focus on becoming the best version of yourself, all other parts of your life fall into line. Priorities become more apparent when you see how they either build you up or simply distract you from what's truly important. Purpose reveals itself, as you know that you are living the best version of yourself and applying it to the betterment of the world.

Things that we think will fulfill us, the souvenirs and trophies we chase, are just things that come and go. However, the lessons we learn and the wisdom we earn through personal development are the real treasures that benefit us beyond goal achievement. If we place developing our personality above the esoteric chasing of success, we will always find meaning and fulfillment.

When we begin to understand ourselves better by way of personal development, we honor our inner yearnings as indicators of our authentic purpose. We learn to approach our potential with an open heart of acceptance and optimism, honoring our purpose and place in the matrix of life. As we begin to experience success, the blossoming of our self-worth allows the full bounty of the Universe to flow into our existence. New challenges give us opportunities to expand our personal mindset, and we approach them with playful wonderment.

If you knew you would not fail, what would you do?

How different would you view your life?

Action puts you in the driver's seat.

Have you ever noticed some people seem to accomplish so much, while others can't seem to get anything done? This is even more apparent when you realize that no one gets more than twenty-four hours in their day. Action creates the tangible; as much as our Think/Feel draws opportunities to us, our actions are often the deciding factor in what manifests for us.

Action aligns your physical and mental energies with your desires. It creates momentum, making it easier to stay on track and maintain your focus. By engaging in activities related to your goals, you signal to the Universe that you are serious about your intentions. This alignment strengthens your Think/Feel powers and point of manifestation, drawing more opportunities and good circumstances to you. Any movement in the direction of your dreams activates manifestation. Even small successes cultivate your self-belief and further clarify your intentions. So, never underestimate your actions, and take some kind of action every day toward your goals. With every step along the way, success will become a natural consequence of your actions.

Alleviate pressure with intentional action.

When you participate in the activities involved in your goals, it keeps movement within your energy. It invigorates your Think/Feel as you continually align your vibrations when you work on the tasks associated with your goals. It keeps you flowing within high vibrations, keeping your potential wide open.

Staying stagnant has greater risks than stepping out of your comfort zone.

Conversely, if you think about but do not act on your goals, you generate stagnant vibrations. When you refuse to do your part or fear the risks involved in stepping out of your comfort zone, your dreams cannot manifest. They eventually shrivel up from inaction. Thinking about action, desperately wishing for action, and even planning for but not taking action are like revving up the engine of your manifestation machine. If you don't take action, it eventually burns out. Don't let that happen to your dreams!

Use practice as the way to overcome procrastination.

Procrastination is a sluggish energy. It first sets in as a coping mechanism, but the longer we allow it to exist, the stronger its hold becomes. Although it can be difficult or scary to begin a new task, remind yourself of a few things:

1. Whatever you begin, you have the option of changing it. Nothing has to be permanent.
2. Nobody knows everything. We all must start somewhere. There is magic in beginning without knowing!
3. Remember that you are simply practicing. With continued practice, you will get better.
4. Action activates manifestation. Any action, even baby steps, will eventually get you there, so take any kind of action to get going.
5. Movement is improvement! Action keeps procrastination at bay or makes it easier to overcome.

WHAT IS ONE TINY STEP TOWARD YOUR GOAL THAT YOU CAN TAKE TODAY?

Don't limit your challenges—challenge your limits.

A common misconception of personal development is that it means we need to do or be better. Yet the core truth of the law of attraction is that we are already whole, a part of the divine Universe. The principles of the law of attraction provide a guiding force to our natural state of being. Personal development, therefore, should be a return to (or revealing of) our natural state of wholeness.

What's required of us is to:

- Honor the wisdom of the principles
- Practice aligning to them
- Remain open to changing our habitual thinking or behaviors
- Replace undesirable behaviors with more productive, positive ones

Sometimes, we need to get out of our comfort zone. Fulfilling our authentic purpose often requires "more" from us. That's the thrilling challenge that, if we don't fully understand the true nature of personal development, can feel overwhelming. Stepping out of our comfort zone is a skill that we can get better at with practice! Especially when we learn that we are capable of so much more than we realize, and when we set aside our need to be perfect and instead humbly open ourselves up to the wonderment of change and growth, becoming the best version of ourselves is a naturally fulfilling practice.

If working on personal development makes you weary, you are doing it wrong.

Consider this: Becoming our best version is not about working on our flaws. It's about honoring our connection to the divine and trusting that we already possess all that we need, all that we must be.

Personal development allows our true nature to do and become what it is meant to be. When we align our divinely appointed inner talents, interests, and experiences to be of service to the world in some capacity (that's yours to figure out), personal development becomes a purposeful, enriching exercise. We (and our ego) just need to step aside and do what the Universe asks of us. Sometimes, that means learning new skills or taking on difficult tasks, but in that process, we find inspiration, direction, and encouragement from the Universe—and that provides motivation to keep growing.

Instead of working on yourself, consider instead the idea of acceptance.

Perfection is not necessary to being the best that we can be. In fact, trying for perfection gets in the way of allowing the Universe to work through us. As we obsess over every perceived fault, we are dishonoring the whole of our being, our connection to the divine. Learning to humbly accept ourselves, flaws and all, is part of opening our soul to our purpose. It's in this open state of wonderment and aligned energy that we discover the bounty of life with unlimited ways to enjoy living. As our consciousness opens to the boundless powers of the Universe, we begin to understand why our soul chose our physical form to explore this life journey and experience all that it means to be human. That is personal development in its most authentic, enriching form.

Examples

Wishes are not enough.

Connor aspired to illustrate children's books. For years, he wished a publishing company would discover his talents and hire him. He visualized it and wrote affirmations, but to no avail. Eventually, he decided that manifestation doesn't work because he did not get what he wished for.

What Connor neglected to understand was the importance of action. We must do our part and take the necessary actions. Once he realized what was missing, he began to take intentional actions. He carefully filled his portfolio with samples of projects that he wanted to do and posted to social media regularly.

After some time, an agent came upon his social media account and reached out to represent him! This collaboration started to bring in professional assignments that kept Connor busy and fulfilled.

Dreams can only work when we work the dreams! So, stop wishing, make a plan for action, and begin! This will demonstrate that you respect your goals enough to try. The Universe can then respond in kind.

Inaction burns out your manifestation engine.

Maybe someday, Kerry thought. *When the kids are grown, when the house is paid for maybe then I'll be able to take action on my dream of starting my own business.*

Over the years, Kerry felt the calling, but time after time, she came up with excuses for why "now" was not the right time. Year after year, her desire lingered, along with her long list of excuses. She attended weekend retreats, participating in all kinds of vision board activities, goal achievement plans, and even one-on-one coaching sessions, but afterward, she would go back to normal life without taking any tangible steps toward activating her dream.

After years of thinking, dreaming, and planning, Kerry decided it was too late. She spoke of her dream with regret and accepted the idea (excuse) that she would never realize it. The real shame is while she gives up on her goal, the world is left without her unique contribution.

Even if you think it's too late, there is still time to take action (until it is too late, if you know what I mean). Don't overthink; just do it.

What are you going to do?

The Wonderment of AUTHENTICITY

Instead of identifying things that you need to improve, make a list of several things that you do exceptionally well.

How can you stop working on yourself and instead simply let your authentic talents shine through?

Take a moment to ponder the possibilities.

Authenticity Is a Superpower

Being true to your own personality, values, and spirit is the most powerful thing you can do. Here's why: The Universe operates with extreme transparency. Because we manifest what we Think/Feel, we need to operate from a place of truth and authenticity. It might feel a bit overwhelming, especially at first. But it can be done, and as you experience the positive effects, you will see how it dramatically improves your experience, which will provide you with more incentive to live in greater authenticity.

Authenticity is empowering; as we uncover our real, honest personal motivations, it frees us from other people's expectations or standards. Instead of chasing the "shoulda, woulda, coulda" things—you know, the symbols of wealth, fancy cars, flashy partners, or other accouterments of success that we're supposed to want—the Universe demands that we get real. It operates on our deep-seated intentions created by our continual thoughts and feelings, including our belief system and sense of worthiness (the deep truths, not the façade we create). The law of attraction operates with honesty, which means we must become authentic with ourselves first.

There is no cheat code or shortcut to the soul work required. And I invite you to consider this: when it comes to our authentic happiness and satisfaction, why would we cheat ourselves out of the process? If we operated from a "get rich quick" mentality, how would we ever learn the truth about our authentic happiness and sincere potential?

Working with the Universe to manifest our dreams begins with the commitment to respect—first and foremost—ourselves and our life journey. How can we respect anyone else, or even the Universe itself, if we don't honor our own interests, truths, and desires?

In essence, the Universe wants us to uncover our truths, release our earthbound inhibitions, and allow our true natures, our souls, to shine beautifully and in full spectrum. It's as if the Universe is simply and lovingly asking us to be exactly who we were born to be. When we tap into our authentic selves and have the courage to live from that place, we will experience true happiness and satisfaction that the shoulda-woulda-couldas will never create. And from that place of authentic joy, we can experience a tidal wave of manifestation, as the Universe will finally be able to deliver all that we are meant to receive.

When you are true to yourself, the right people and opportunities are naturally drawn to you.

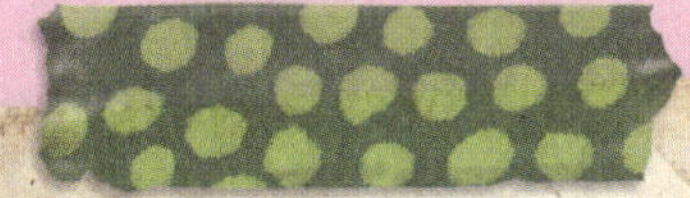

What's one thing you wished more people knew about you?

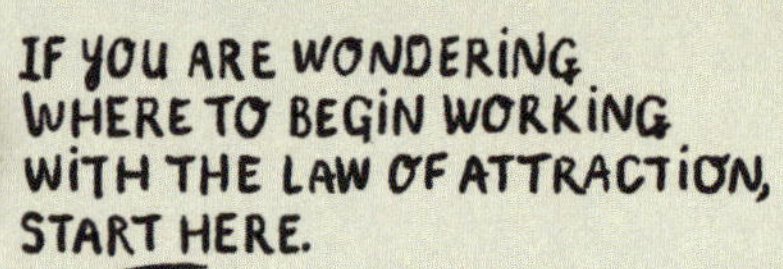

IF YOU ARE WONDERING WHERE TO BEGIN WORKING WITH THE LAW OF ATTRACTION, START HERE.

The Possibility Puerta

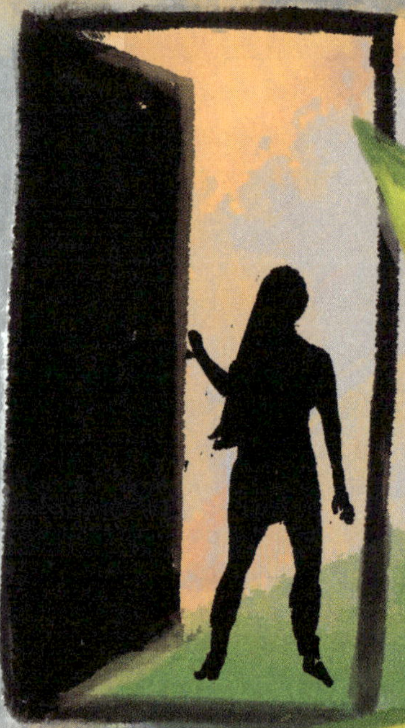

Most of us hope that someday, we will be good enough, blessed with or worthy of the life of our dreams. The concept of "someday" is ambiguous and counterintuitive to the law of attraction, which requires us to allow our greatest good to flow now.

According to the law of attraction, we are inherently capable and worthy of all our hopes and dreams as soon as we allow them to flow into our existence. It is not from judgment of our worthiness, because the law of attraction doesn't work like that. It simply responds in kind to what we emit via our Think/Feel (remember, we can't fake it). If we refuse to accept who we are or if we hide behind arrogance, pride, shame, or fear, we vibrate at low frequencies, and the Universe will respond with similar vibrations.

We do not have to remain imprisoned by our past or perceived flaws. We are humans, being and doing the best that we can. Learning to accept ourselves as is doesn't require us to be perfect. We can be works in progress and still manifest strongly.

In fact, with the open mindset of humility, we are powerfully connected to the Universe! When we see self-improvement as a process of acceptance first, we keep our souls open to our greatest potential. Because of the now dynamic of the Universe, as soon as we begin to release our self-imposed limitations, we shift our energy, which will immediately recalibrate our vibrations.

The Possibility Puerta opens just as soon as you decide to allow your soul to wonder at your own potential. Open that door and walk through!

Acceptance
Humility
Wonderment
Curiosity
Surrender
Future
Possibilities
Adventure
Potential

Circle which word resonates the most with you

The Wonderment of POSSIBILITY

How would your past have been different had you believed in your abilities instead of worrying about your flaws?

Now, how can you take this wisdom and realign your future with it?

Authenticity Thumbprint

Like a thumbprint, we are each comprised of a varied mix of talents, skills, and interests that makes us unique. Finding your authenticity is about identifying the core attributes that are closest to your heart, then finding ways to express those traits.

This exercise provides a framework for you to understand what makes you unique. It is also useful for identifying connections between different interests of yours, which point to ways that you can combine interests to create work, hobby, or volunteer opportunities that are perfectly aligned to your authentic personality. The closer they align, the more meaningful and satisfying they will be!

The following page is a worksheet that will help clarify your Authenticity Thumbprint. In the four squares around the center heart, list your absolute favorite things to think about, your favorite activities, or your favorite special interests. If you're not sure of your favorites, just list the things that you do most often (you can change these around as you work through this exercise). Write in pencil so you can erase and revise as you go.

DO YOU SEE HOW THIS EXERCISE CAN HELP YOU PINPOINT THE UNIQUE WAYS THAT YOU CAN EXPRESS WHAT MAKES YOU AUTHENTICALLY YOU?

Then, in all the surrounding squares, list other interests, work activities, skills, etc. that you have. After you have all the squares filled up with things, rearrange them as you identify items that could relate to one another. Think creatively about how you could connect seemingly random interests to find ways to express your unique combination of traits.

Here are two examples of how the Authenticity Thumbprint works:

1. If you wrote in one square that you love dogs and in another one that you like to run, maybe you can connect them. Your favorite way of giving back could be exercising dogs at the local animal shelter.
2. In your center heart, you wrote that you love makeup tutorials. Next to it, you listed your current job as a hair stylist, and in another box, you wrote that you love to perform. Through this exercise, you could realize that your Authenticity Thumbprint would be to create your own social media business helping others learn about the beauty industry. Or your dream job could be working in the theater or movie industry or in commercial photography as a photo stylist.

Authenticity Thumbprint Clarifier

To reach a port we must sail,
sometimes with the wind, and
sometimes against it. But we
must not drift or lie at anchor.
~ Oliver Wendell Holmes Sr.

WONDER
AT IT ALL

MANIFESTATION
MAGNETISM
UNIVERSAL (EXPANDING) INFLUENCE
UNWAVERING (PURE) DESIRE
RIGHT (CONSCIENTIOUS) ACTION
HARMONY
DELICATE BALANCE (PARADOXICAL INTENT)
The Law of Attraction
PLEASE NOTE: I HAVE INCLUDED ALTERNATIVE NAMES IN PARENTHESES

Part Two

THE SEVEN PRINCIPLES

LAND HO!

We have arrived at the second part of this book.

The law of attraction is a collection of seven principles that impact and contribute to your life experience. By understanding the wisdom of each principle, you can create a systematic, spiritual structure for living that will nurture and strengthen your manifestation power.

With curious, open-minded wonderment, let's explore the lush details of the seven life-changing principles that comprise the law of attraction.

WHAT YOU focus UPON
EXPANDS iN YOUR REALiTY

PRINCIPLE ONE

MANIFESTATION

According to this principle, we can manifest (create) our reality through the power of our thoughts, feelings, and beliefs. Reality is a perception of our consciousness. What is visible in our reality is first invisible—by way of our thoughts, imaginations, and awareness. Our consciousness, and what we choose to focus on, is our choice.

Manifestation teaches us that whatever we consistently focus on will expand in our awareness. Our choice of focus via our Think/Feel targets our manifestation energy, drawing to us matching vibrations. Therefore, our reality is the result of our focus.

This occurs intentionally or unintentionally, depending on whether we are aware of the cause and effect of our focus. The key to successfully applying this principle is consistently, intentionally focusing on what you desire. Find ways to think about and act on your goals every day to activate the Universe's energy toward them.

Because of its authentic nature, the Universe does not judge, interpret, or edit manifestations. Therefore, be very mindful to focus on what you want instead of worrying about what you don't! You will manifest precisely the kind of energy that you continually think and emotionally resonate with.

Our Focus Becomes Our Legacy

The first principle is the cornerstone of the law of attraction. It is the core recognition that your consciousness is a choice that you make. You manifest what you expect, whether it's positive or negative.

Your mind filters and prioritizes information based on your attention. What you focus on is what you tend to notice. It's a basic psychological phenomenon. Your focus is like a lens through which you interpret and interact with the world. But the law of attraction takes it a step further by declaring that you manifest, or bring into your reality, what you choose to focus on. What you consistently focus on affects your beliefs, emotions, actions, and, consequently, the opportunities and experiences you attract. Seeing the positive encourages more positivity. Negativity attracts more things to feel negative about.

The law of attraction reflects matching vibrations, situations, or opportunities that resonate in the spectrum of your Think/Feel. As you practice consistently focusing on positive aspects of life, your brain will be attuned to opportunities and experiences that match that positivity. When you believe in the possibility of success and focus on achieving it, you are more likely to take the necessary actions to make it a reality.

Conversely, if you focus on failure (or worry, fear, etc.), guess what you'll notice? Negativity resonates with similar vibrations, drawing into your life matching vibrations of negativity. This happens even when you do it unintentionally from an undercurrent of anxiety or doubt by way of your Think/Feel (remember the authentic nature of the Universe).

But with continued practice, you can train your brain to focus with intention. What you choose to see is a self-fulfilling prophecy! The choices you make every day either build your self-belief or inhibit your growth, shaping the course of your life.

The importance of your daily focus cannot be overstated. Each thought and connected emotion sends out a vibration that will connect with similar energies. Day in and day out, these thoughts and emotions compound with every experience, eventually defining your life.

When you are elderly and look back on your life, what do you hope to have experienced?

How can you recalibrate your current focus to make that happen?

If you want to improve your life experience, it begins here with this simple yet profound principle. Becoming aware of your habitual focus will help you understand what you are manifesting and why you are manifesting it in your reality.

Examples

The Universe will deliver what you Think/ Feel intentionally or unintentionally.

Caroline was a program director for a state university. Her job kept her too busy, and she wished for a less stressful situation. She constantly daydreamed about retiring. Her plan was to retire in several years, except in her daydreams, she envisioned herself living retired life in the present moment. Every day as she commuted to work, she thought about how she would rather spend her early morning at home with her dog and a good book. The fantasy stayed with her throughout her workday.

One day, Caroline was notified that her program was being eliminated after the current spring semester. The news came as a shock to her! It was several years too soon for her retirement plans. Yet her insistent daydreams, in a metaphysical sense, had been signaling her authentic desire for retirement now and, consequently, had brought her wish to fruition.

Learning how to ask the Universe for exactly what we want is critical to manifesting our dreams. When you find yourself daydreaming about something, ask yourself, "Do I really want this to manifest as I am currently envisioning it?"

Get precise with your focus.

I have used the word abundance as my chosen mantra for years, and keeping a small image with me as a reminder of my manifestation focus on abundance has worked amazingly well. I have manifested massive amounts of abundance—financial abundance by way of prosperity and an abundance of happiness by way of relationships. I have come to realize that abundance has attributes to it that I didn't know would manifest, like clutter (a.k.a. an abundance of things)!

I laughingly must acknowledge I allowed a broad definition of abundance into my reality, and it continuously served it up in all corners of my home. So, as I've gotten better and better at manifestation, I've learned to define with more precision. I now use my visualization practice to identify what kind of abundance I wish to create. Understanding how the Universe works, I know that I can hone in on the exact way I want it to deliver my wishes.

The sharper my focus, the stronger and more accurate my manifestation.

How to Sharpen Your Focus

First, you must understand what you truly want. Because of the authentic nature of the Universe, you must be clear with your desires and goal achievement.

Find ways to connect your Think/Feel to the achievement of success to fully integrate it into your psyche and soul. Release the "how" and just joyfully daydream about your aspirations. Keep your Think/Feel light and free by reminding yourself to stay in playful wonder.

Spend time every day visualizing what you want; make it a sacred practice that you repeat throughout the day. The more that you can send vibrations into the Universe, the stronger and swifter your manifestation will be.

Continue to practice your manifestation process. Read about it, think about it, speak about it, and plan, visualize, and play with your dreams. Find as many ways as you can to integrate the process into your psyche and soul. As you become more aware of the manifestation process shaping your life, you can become more mindful of your active part in manifestation. And with practice, you will get better at intentionally shaping your Think/Feel focus.

Remember to feed your focus to starve out the less desirable. This takes continual improvement, identifying what you like and putting your focus there, reaching for a more authentic Think/Feel. Innately, your Think/Feel will improve as you apply more attention to the thoughts and feelings that you want to experience.

Take some moments to become aware of your thought process and what you notice in your life.

Ask yourself, "Is this what I want to experience? Am I noticing all the many blessings already in my life? How can I remind myself of or shift my focus to positivity?"

Awareness is progress.

When you become aware of this manifestation principle, you will see examples of it in your current life. This is amazing progress, as you become more sensitive to what you want versus what you don't. Some are good events, and some are not. Celebrate every instance of awareness as progress that you're learning how to identify your Think/Feel and manifest with intention.

Your Think/Feel begins to shift.

Everyone's life is a series of events. We all have our own share of challenges, fears, hopes, and disappointments. That is part of the human condition! But how we perceive and react to our life events is what impacts our enjoyment of them. Whether we see the good or bad will determine what we manifest going forward.

So, instead of worrying about the things that may go wrong, we are better served by shifting to an empowered mindset of looking for the solutions to the inevitable decisions that we need to make. That small shift in attitude takes us out of the reactionary, weakened emotional position of victimhood. When you can see your thought process as solution-based, you will notice more opportunities, options, and ultimately the positive aspects of every situation.

You know manifestation is beginning to work when . . .

You begin to see objects or topics related to your goals and desires everywhere.

You have a heightened intuition. For example, you turn when someone is looking at you or you sense that you are going to find a parking spot up front and a car leaves a space just as you pull up.

You trust your instincts instead of processing everything through your intellect.

Life becomes a fun game of finding evidence of manifestation. It's everywhere!

You feel déjà vu or goose bumps before something important happens. It's a physical reaction that you are becoming spiritually attuned to the Universe's request to "pay attention!"

Materialize Your Dreams

Draw a picture of yourself accomplishing your goal.

In detail, describe it as precisely as you can.

Visualize Success

What personality traits will support the achievement of your goals—new skills, experiences, etc.? Describe them as precisely as you can.

What will this success feel like?

KEEP THIS VISUALIZATION DAYDREAM FUN. IT'S RECESS FROM STRESS!

THIS IS THE TIME TO IMAGINE WITH A CHILDLIKE SENSE OF WONDERMENT, NOT THE TIME TO OVERTHINK THE PROCESS.

WHEN YOU LOOK AT YOUR VISION YOU WANT TO SEND OUT PURE, FULL-OF-POSSIBILITY VIBES.

LIKE ATTRACTS LIKE

PRINCIPLE TWO

MAGNETISM

Everything that exists has energy. You radiate energy even if you are unaware of it. And you attract and are attracted to similar, familiar, or matching energy forces. Everything that is in your life—people, things, and opportunities, as well as the circumstances in which you find yourself—is the result of Magnetism.

We can intentionally improve our life situations by harnessing the powers of Magnetism. When we begin to emit a more intentional, focused energy, we can improve what and who is attracted to our life experience. By choosing what we think about and being mindful of our corresponding emotions—our Think/Feel—we can intentionally target the energy we emit and therefore attract into our life.

If you want to improve your life, relationships, or opportunities be mindful of your own energy and align it with success.

Be the Energy You Wish to Receive

Dr. Wayne Dyer succinctly stated, "You attract what you are, not what you want."

We bring into our reality vibrations that match our authentic Think/Feel. We are attracted to—and attractive to—matching vibrations. What connects are our similarly resonating vibrations. That's what friends mean when they say, "We just clicked." There is a familiarity, a sense of recognition at some level. Energy speaks volumes, more so than actions, words, or even physical demeanors. Our energy vibration impacts our love relationships, career, friendships, and opportunities that manifest.

When we resonate with the same vibration as our goals do, we attract it to our existence. The right people and situations seem to pop up out of nowhere! We meet someone new, and we instantly feel a connection. Our dream home becomes available just when we start to look for real estate. The synergy is remarkable when we are in a state of aligned vibrations.

What came first, the chicken or the egg? This philosophical question demonstrates the foundational principle of Magnetism. If you want to be happy, you must first identify things that make you happy. If you want to find love, understand what love means to you, nurturing these attributes in yourself so that you become a vibrational match.

Authenticity opens the Possibility Puerta to our greatest potential.

Instead of thinking that something outside of you will make you happy, this principle requires you to understand your part in manifestation. You must become what you seek. It's not always about doing more; it's simply about being more authentic, and the right things will present themselves as a result. When you operate from a place of authenticity, you will open up the possibilities of the law of attraction that align with your intentions.

This is where the concept of personal development connects with manifestation. Achieving your goals becomes easier when you focus your efforts on becoming the you that your successful achievement needs. In endeavoring to be your best self, you will attract what naturally aligns. Oftentimes, what manifests is beyond your original dreams!

Think for a moment about what you wish to see in other people.

How can you begin to mirror those characteristics in yourself?

**Attract what you expect,
reflect what you desire,
become what you respect,
mirror what you admire.
~unknown**

Examples

Relationships are the ultimate mirrors.

Carli often lamented that she could not find a good man to settle down with her. She repeatedly found herself in relationships with noncommittal partners.

Her longest relationship was tumultuous. Her boyfriend's unwillingness to commit frustrated her, so she would break up with him, only to return to him after a week or so.

As the saying goes, "It takes two to tango," and this dysfunctional dance mystified and frustrated Carli. Although she didn't exhibit noncommittal tendencies, she was quick to pull away, break up, and then get back together. Her energetic vibration was indecisive, similar to or matching that of her noncommittal companion.

As she confronted her part in this dysfunction, Carli began to feel empowered to make the necessary changes. She ended her relationship and stuck with that decision, and she spent the next year improving her Think/Feel and visualizing her ideal partner. She thought about the traits she wished for in a partner and focused on developing compatible traits within herself.

When Carli met the man who would become her husband, she immediately felt a connection with him. Because of the soulful work that she had done on herself, she recognized his similar vibration and felt a familiarity of intentional alignment. He was the right match to her energy—a match made via the law of attraction.

Donny wanted more happiness but felt stuck at a job he disliked.

His colleagues were negative, constantly complaining about work. Every Friday, they would get together for happy hour and spend the entire time gossiping and griping about the week.

As Donny began to implement the law of attraction in his life, he became painfully aware of how depleting it was to his spirit to be around his coworkers. He realized their negative energy rubbed off on him, damaging his attitude and, consequently, his vibrations.

He finally decided that his mental, emotional, and manifestational health could not improve if he continued engaging in other people's negativity. He started working on improving his mindset first. This involved a continual process of catching himself thinking negatively or looking for faults in other people or situations, and replacing these thoughts with improved ideas. He implemented the principle of Magnetism by focusing on being the kind of energy he wanted to experience. It required him to create boundaries from those who were overly negative.

As Donny practiced the principles of the law of attraction, his mood lifted, except when he attended the Friday gripe fests. So, he enrolled in a course to improve his career skills, focusing his evenings on this productive endeavor instead.

After Donny successfully earned his course certificate, he found a much better job surrounded by supportive colleagues. His whole life took on more meaning as he continued to choose his authentic happiness instead of allowing negativity to impact his experiences.

How to Ride the Waves of Ever-Expanding Magnetism

Attracting what we desire is a process of aligning ourselves to the vibration of it, then allowing Magnetism to bring to us situations, opportunities, and other things that match in energy.

Alignment is a process of determining what vibrations resonate with the same energy as our goals. Determine what mindset and skills are compatible, and work to incorporate them into your Think/Feel. As you work with Magnetism, ask yourself, "What attributes support that energy?"

Allowing means that, instead of feeling overwhelmed, we trust the opportunities that flow our way as a direct result of our Think/Feel, and we can adjust the course and currency of the flow by adjusting our Think/Feel vibrations. The Universe will always respond in kind.

Be mindful of the new opportunities and people that enter your life. How are they connected to your practice of Magnetism? Stay aware of your alignment with your authentic desires, reaching for opportunities that come your way. Expect good things to follow! This repetitive practice of aligning, attracting, allowing, and achieving will expand with every successful cycle. Remaining humble and open to change keeps the Possibility Puerta wide open. When we see life as full of wonder and nuanced adventure, we position our Think/Feel in the direction of high vibrations of wonderment. Even when we may not know exactly what we are supposed to do or be to attract our goals, the Universe can provide guidance at a welcoming frequency.

When we always seek better, we keep our hearts and minds open to better. This doesn't mean we are never satisfied; in fact, it means the exact opposite! Seeking better means we are overjoyed with what we have and who we are, and we know that there is even more out there for us! That delicious prospect is what keeps us open to unlimited potential.

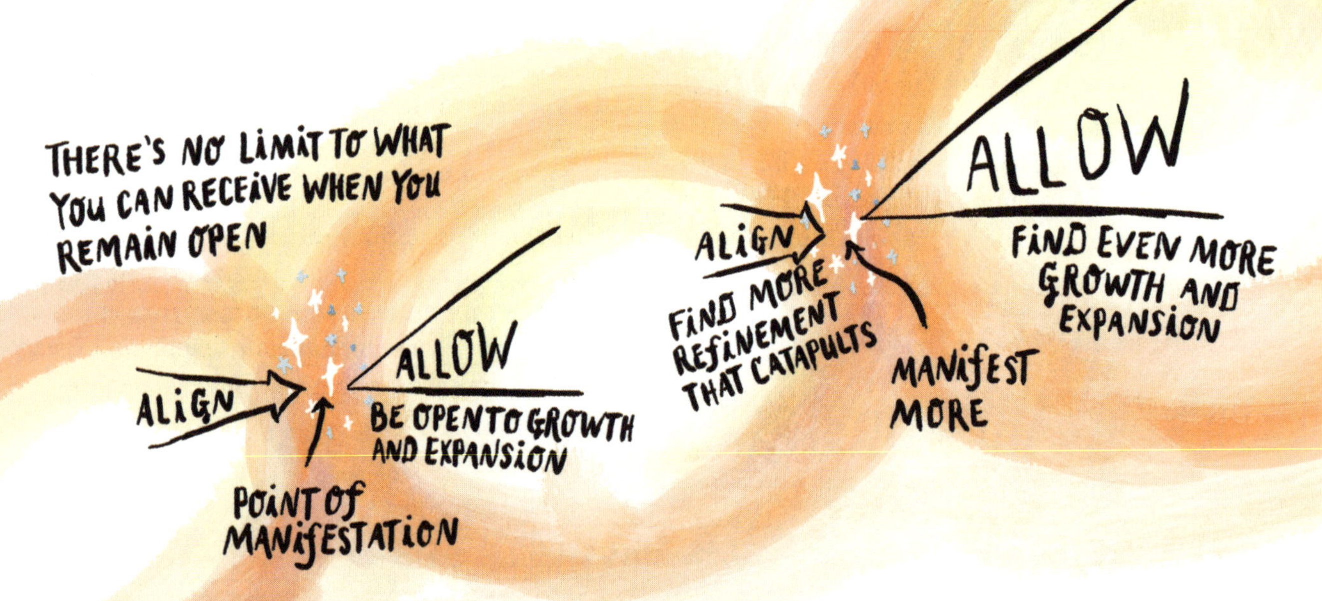

Don't chase. Attract.

There is a delicate balance between working on ourselves (and our goals) and attracting with a sense of confidence. It is important to understand the difference between chasing and attracting.

Chasing happens when we try to shortcut the inner development of alignment. Many of us were taught that accomplishment takes hard work. We mistakenly believe that means utilizing all our energy, personal drive, and determination to chase, or force, goal achievement and personal development. We think we have to hustle—just the sound of that word can be exhausting!

Rather than seeing our goals separate from our true nature or requiring domination of others, we bring our goals and dreams to us by attracting them. The work this requires is inner work, deciding what we authentically desire and visualizing successful completion of it and opening ourselves in the process. Then incorporating the attributes that will bring it to us by way of our actions. This may require learning new skills, practicing new habits, or getting out of our comfort zone, but the work should be invigorating and soul fulfilling, not draining or domineering. It is personal development work that allows us to blossom into the most successful versions of ourselves.

Attracting from our authentic selves is easier and infinitely more powerful than chasing.

You know Magnetism is working when . . .

You can see and touch the items pertaining to your goal. For example, you are shopping, and the exact object of your desire is displayed in a shop window. Go try it on, take it for a test drive, or feel it with pure wonder and remind yourself, *This will be mine soon.*

The job promotion or opportunity that you want suddenly becomes available.

You become aware of how other people's energies align with or go against your own.

The people you once desperately hoped would like you no longer appeal to you. As your vibration improves, you will not accept anything less than authentic connection.

You begin to meet new, interesting, and more enlightened people.

Becoming Your Best Version

In the following columns, write ten words that describe your ideal way of life.

	HEALTH	FINANCES	PERSONAL LIFE
1.			
2.			
3.			
4.			
5.			
6.			
7.			
8.			
9.			
10.			

These words represent your favorite attributes and authentic aspirations. Your goals and personal development work should lead to or support these ideas.

Now take these words and write them in the silhouette on the next page. Color the rest of the picture, and enjoy thinking about becoming the best version of you!

I AM

WHEN YOU GO...
...GO ALL IN

PRINCIPLE THREE

UNWAVERING DESIRE

Your desire to achieve or attract a certain goal must be strong and consistent for the goal to manifest. Your desire should be so powerful that it becomes a driving force behind your actions and decisions. If you focus on your goal with a full commitment to success, obstacles and setbacks will not sway you.

Conversely, if your goals are not very well defined, your results will be of a similar frequency—weak or not quite right. The Universe cannot edit the frequency of your energy, so if you have doubts about your goals, they will not manifest properly.

To activate manifestation, focus your Think/Feel. Use wonderment to visualize all the possibilities with open-minded, unfiltered clarity.

Nurture authentically believing in your ability to achieve your goals, and then the Universe can return the vibrations with the path to the goals' fulfillment.

Like a Beacon, Draw Your Goals to You

Light beams from a lighthouse pulse steadily to alert and guide ships. Unwavering Desire does something similar. Every time you think about a goal of yours, it casts a beacon of desire, drawing to you matching vibrations. This principle explains the importance of maintaining a steady and consistent beacon of vibration so that the Universe can track it.

If your Think/Feel is unsteady and inconsistent, it will be like a beam of light flashing here, then over there, and then not at all. Do you see how difficult that is to track?

Unwavering Desire teaches us the importance of maintaining a consistent, strong Think/Feel regarding our goals. With each thought, we have the power to direct our vibrations with precise intensity, and as long as we stay steady and true, the Universe can connect to them, bringing our desires to us.

It is important that you stay consistent with your desires, which can be nurtured with the exercises that I have included in this book. It is intuitive; doing the soulful work keeps you emitting the right energy. As your goals become clearer and more authentic, your beacon of desire will get stronger and more consistent, too.

How will learning to believe in yourself improve your goal achievement and your life in general?

What can you do every day to instill Unwavering Desire for your goals?

Examples

Belief is a choice.

Sarah struggled with self-doubt and a lack of confidence. She often felt like she wasn't good enough in various aspects of her life, including her career, relationships, and personal goals, which kept her from being her authentic self. So, she decided that she wanted to change this and develop her self-belief.

She began by letting go of perfection and choosing to reach for acceptance. She put together a very detailed list of goals and skills she personally wanted to gain. And she joined a support group of like-minded people, who continually reminded her of her goals and strengths as she courageously started learning to believe in herself.

Along the way, Sarah realized how important it was for her to focus her Think/Feel in the direction she wanted to go. She eliminated doubt by applying layers of self-love. With every milestone she successfully reached, she celebrated the progress she was making. As she accomplished some of her smaller goals, it bolstered her belief in her abilities, and it impressed her friends; they asked her how she was making these changes. As she coached them, she realized it helped her too!

Belief, Sarah learned, is a choice and something she could improve with practice. Accomplishing goals took knowledge, but the most important element was belief that she could change for the better.

Chelsey wanted to run a marathon.

Even though she wasn't an athlete, she wanted to prove to herself that she could take on the ambitious goal of running a full marathon. She identified the race that she wanted to accomplish and created a training program up to that date. She decided to keep a journal documenting every training run, her time and performance, and track her mindset along the way, focusing on her successes to feed her motivation.

About three months before her marathon, she experienced a particularly difficult run. She came home exhausted and dejected. She thought, *How will I be able to run a marathon when I don't feel like I am improving?*

Then she sat down to record her time, distance, and emotions in her journal. She reviewed her previous journal entries and noticed something very important. Two weeks prior, she had been elated about her training, yet her time and distance were much less impressive than the stats from her most recent run.

"I am improving!" she realized, her emotions instantly lifting. She was more exhausted today partly because she was running faster for longer distances. If she hadn't been tracking her progress, she may not have realized that. This bolstered her confidence, just what she needed at this critical point in her training.

Documenting her success journey was the exact thing that built Chelsey's belief along the way. She carried this wisdom with her when she crossed the finish line three months later, and into her life going forward. She knew she could accomplish anything that she wanted by focusing on her success and intentionally believing in herself.

How to Nurture Unwavering Desire by Bridging the Gap

Since the Universe operates from our truths, Unwavering Desire is a critical piece of our manifestations. At times, a gap may exist between our aspirations and our belief that we can make them happen—particularly for the things we want the most. Intense longings tap into our deeply held beliefs and inner thoughts, sometimes bumping against our sense of worthiness.

No matter where you are right now on the sliding scale of self-perceived worthiness, you can improve your ability to soulfully, humbly, and joyfully receive. First, give yourself a moment of grace. We are each on a path of self-love. The journey to reach the best version of yourself is paved with forgiveness, especially for yourself. It may take time to reboot your self-belief, but it will lead to life-altering improvements.

Let's examine the belief/worthiness issue as it pertains to manifestation. When we question our worthiness, we emit a low frequency, such as fear, worry, or doubt, which, according to the principles of the law of attraction, will attract more fear, worry, or doubt. Because the Universe reflects what we put out, we need to mind the gap between our desired reality and our current mindset.

Now that you understand the connections between your Think/Feel and the manifestation of your reality, you can begin to understand the pragmatic importance and soul-enriching practice of learning how to believe in your true potential. What manifests is a result of setting aside your ego (the part of you that doubts your worth) and using curious wonderment to open your potential and allow the Universe to flow through you without question or judgment, trusting what shows up is meant to be. It's not so much about having all the answers; it's about trusting that inspiration (your connection to the Universe's wisdom) will provide what you need, when you need it, for the greater good.

You can nurture this state of mind when you think about developing your sense of worthiness as a practice. You can practice anything that you want to improve, whether it is a skill or a thought process, like developing a healthier self-belief. Regularly connect with your goals and visualize successful attainment of them. Envision the personality attributes you are developing as you work toward your goals. Celebrate every success no matter how humble. Find others doing similar things and learn from them.

Reinforce self-belief with affirmations.

Affirmations are positive statements that, when repeated, can help build your self-belief. As you repeat an affirmation, you begin to imprint it into your Think/Feel, thereby activating the manifestation process. But in order to work, the affirmation, most importantly, must be believable. So, as you create an affirmation, think about how you can word it so that you can achieve an authentic feeling of believability.

You can use the worksheet on the following page to craft believable affirmations. But if you're wondering how to begin using effective, believable affirmations to reshape your mindset, here is my favorite affirmation to start with:

"I am ________________ in the making."

Fill in the blank with who you will be when you successfully achieve your goal (such as a marathon runner, a happy romantic partner, or a successful businessperson—whoever you will be upon achieving your goal). "In the making" means that you are in the process of figuring things out; it implies action. Knowing you don't have to have all the answers now reduces worry and pressure.

By filling in the you that you will be upon successful completion, you will begin to identify with that new version of you. Remember, the more we can connect and identify with our goal, the more likely we will stick with the tasks necessary to make it our reality, and the easier it will be for the Universe to connect and deliver.

You are on the right track with Unwavering Desire when . . .

Your Think/Feel consistently resonates in the direction of your dreams.

You catch yourself worrying (or doubting), but you stop and shift back to a better manifestation Think/Feel. Awareness is progress.

You can see the path to your successful achievement.

New opportunities begin to appear, and you instinctively know which ones will get you closer to your goal.

You look forward to working on your goals because it feels good, not overwhelming.

You begin to feel different and make changes (a new hairstyle, clothing style, or career choice). It's an external manifestation of the changes you are making within.

As you believe in better, you reach for better.

Believable, Achievable Affirmations

1. Start it with "I" and make it personal.
2. Make it present tense, as if it already exists.
3. Frame it in a positive tone. Focus on what you want (not on what you don't want).
4. Make sure it is believable to you now.
5. Choose words that are precise and descriptive.

You can choose an affirmation that feels believable now, and as you improve and progress, you can adjust your affirmation to stretch it further. Think of it as a ladder; you reach for the next rung as you go.

I AM ______________________

What is your goal or desired outcome?
How will you feel when you achieve it?
What actions do you need to take?

- [ ] Is it written from a positive perspective?
- [ ] Is it believable to you now?
- [ ] Does it spark joy when you read it?

Create several different affirmations to understand how you Think/Feel about them. Compare and contrast how the affirmations resonate with you. Choose whichever one is the strongest.

Put your favorite one here:

Keep your affirmation near you so that you are continuously reminded of it.

The Wonderment of REPETITION

Repetition imprints the message in your psyche. The more you repeat something, the more you believe it. So, look at your affirmation, visualizing it with open wonderment, as often as possible. Feel its success; practice resonating with the vibration of success. Remind yourself that that is the "you" waiting to be realized.

YOU BECOME
WHAT
YOU BELIEVE.
SO BELIEVE IN YOUR BEST

TRUST THE
UNIVERSE

PRINCIPLE FOUR

DELICATE BALANCE

Everything in life is interconnected. The Universe is comprised of various forces and elements that balance one another. When the different aspects of your life are in balance, manifestation flows, and you feel centered and peaceful.

All aspects of life come into play with this principle: physical, mental, emotional, and spiritual. To achieve a sense of well-being and fulfillment, we must strive to maintain balance among different aspects of our life experience. That includes our Think/Feel connection to our goals and dreams. We must strike a balance between our strong desire for those goals and our patience with the Universe's divine timing. This means maintaining trust when things don't manifest exactly as we want, staying open to alternative (maybe better) opportunities.

Trust that the Universe will provide exactly what you need at the right time. Do your part while allowing the Universe to do its part, too.

The Delicate Balance of Effort and Ease

As previously mentioned, taking action is a crucial component of activating manifestation. You need to actively work toward your goals, whether that's through setting intentions, making plans, or putting in the necessary work. Action aligns your physical and mental energies with your desires and helps you move closer to them. This principle, Delicate Balance, further defines the kind of action that opens you up to the law of attraction. When you find the ease in action, you adjust your energy to be receptive, following the inspiration that is available to you in any situation. When you're relaxed, open to joyful wonderment, and not obsessively attached to outcomes, you create space for the Universe to work on your behalf.

Balancing effort with ease means finding the equilibrium between actively pursuing things and allowing things to unfold. It acknowledges that excessive effort, stress, or unhealthy attachment can interfere with the process of attracting what you desire. It's essential to put in the effort—yet remain in a steady state of open wonderment, trusting the Universe to respond in its own time.

Our role is to stay receptive, allowing the Universe to bring our desires to us.

It's in that Delicate Balance that we learn that we are capable of effort but also worthy of ease. Maintaining balance keeps us both achieving and allowing—and our Possibility Puerta wide open.

Trying harder isn't the answer.

Many of us have been taught that work must be intense and that personal improvement requires us to "feel the burn" physically, mentally, and spiritually. However, working that hard makes us feel overwhelmed, anxious, or exhausted, which, as we have learned, repels positive manifestation. The Universe does not require such intensity; in fact, it responds much better when we do things with a sense of ease. Be mindful of the kind of energy you exert while pursuing your goals. Ease is best! Effort is good, but working through exhaustion is not.

Busyness doesn't equate to success. In fact, to manifest more success may require you to slow down. In that space, you can clarify what truly matters.

The Universe does not punch a time clock.

Time is a human construct, while the Universe is eternal. Our earthly time frame may not matter in the grand scale of things. Learning to respect the timing of the Universe is part of the wisdom of this principle.

We can ask for our dreams to manifest, but if the conditions are not right, those dreams cannot flow into our reality. Sometimes, our faulty practices block the Possibility Puerta. Other times, the Universe delays manifestation, knowing that because of the complex matrix of a myriad of events, our ultimate manifestation may take a different form or timing. Perhaps the Universe has something even grander in store! So, when your timeline doesn't manifest the way you thought, release control to the Universe. Continue the practice of Delicate Balance, and trust the Universe to deliver what is destined.

Examples

Find the ease in effort.

When Jayne began to practice yoga, her instructor encouraged her to find her breath and ease in every movement. Although Jayne diligently tried, she found herself shaky and unable to maintain her position. But with continued practice, she began to understand what the instructor was trying to teach.

Even when learning a new, more advanced pose, Jayne became very mindful of her breath, maintaining an easy cadence. She realized she had previously been holding her breath, and the lack of oxygen caused her to become shaky. Her breath was the key to advancing her practice, and staying in a state of ease within her mind allowed her to explore her poses, flowing from one position to the next.

"Ease" became Jayne's mantra as she grew more and more skilled at her yoga practice. She took this principle into her life beyond the yoga mat, realizing that finding the ease in everything she did allowed her the freedom to explore her truest potential. What manifested was the natural consequence of her intentional practice of ease in her Think/Feel and efforts.

Evelyn grew up with thrifty parents who taught her the value of hard work.

She prided herself on her work ethic and her overflowing weekly schedule, yet secretly, she felt overwhelmed and desperate. She truly believed that she could not take a day off for fear that she would fall behind.

Eventually, after years of intense activity, Evelyn experienced severe burnout. She realized the incessant stress had taken a toll, physically and emotionally. She decided to take drastic action. She slashed everything from her calendar that wasn't necessary because her health was demanding rest and healing. This required her to make tough decisions and eliminate things that she had worked hard to be included in.

Despite her deeply ingrained sense of productivity, Evelyn leaned into the principle of Delicate Balance. She began to replace activity with all-important rest. She prioritized things that refueled her emotional reserves. She spent moments every day visualizing a healthy, balanced, and purposeful life with more ease in her efforts.

The changes Evelyn made within her psyche started to manifest a new reality. Although her schedule was lighter, she realized more success. As her focus shifted to identifying the things that filled her with happiness and gratitude, the Universe served up more things that aligned to her vibrations. Because she wasn't busy chasing everything, she had the mind space to determine the best opportunities based on her desired life experience.

Life wasn't about proving her worth anymore. And the slower pace empowered her to be more mindful of all the blessings already in her life.

How to Detach from Results to Manifest with Ease

One of the most effective ways to nurture Delicate Balance is to eliminate the pressures of achievement. This concept is somewhat counter to what we are told to do. The hustle mentality urges us to push hard all the time, yet the truth is such intensity can repel the manifestation of our goals. So, if you have ever felt exhausted by achievement, you may have inadvertently worked against the principle of Delicate Balance.

Manifestation works by way of our Think/Feel. Too much pressure often results in negative, anxious energy, constricting our vibrations.

Here are some suggestions on how to alleviate this common misstep:

- Break your goals down into achievable tasks. When you have a good plan of action, all you must do is focus on each step, trusting that success will be the natural consequence of your actions.
- Allow yourself more time to explore without pressure to perform. Curiosity and a playful sense of wonderment allow you to see things more objectively—maybe even from a different perspective! Trust your inspiration. It may lead to another path, one that is better than the one you planned.
- Remain emotionally detached from the outcome. Focus your efforts on the actions, habits, and practices that lead up to your goal, but don't obsess about the actual event.

When we want something badly, it is difficult to practice allowing, yet the Universe requires that we loosen our grip on control to manifest with ease. It's a paradox we come to know—learning to manage this Delicate Balance of desire and detachment.

To allow manifestation, it can be helpful to practice detachment from the outcome, thereby eliminating the urge to force or apply too much pressure on your performance. Instead of obsessing about your goal, practice seeing beyond its successful completion. It's a bit like swinging a golf club. To send a golf ball down the fairway, you must focus on hitting the ball, yet your swing must continue its trajectory beyond the point of contact. The follow-through is the key to aiming the golf ball!

The same concept applies here. Focus on your goal, but continue your energy beyond it. The follow-through will keep you from hyperfocusing on the event. Keep a steady and constant energy flow around and through you as the way to maintain the flow of manifestation.

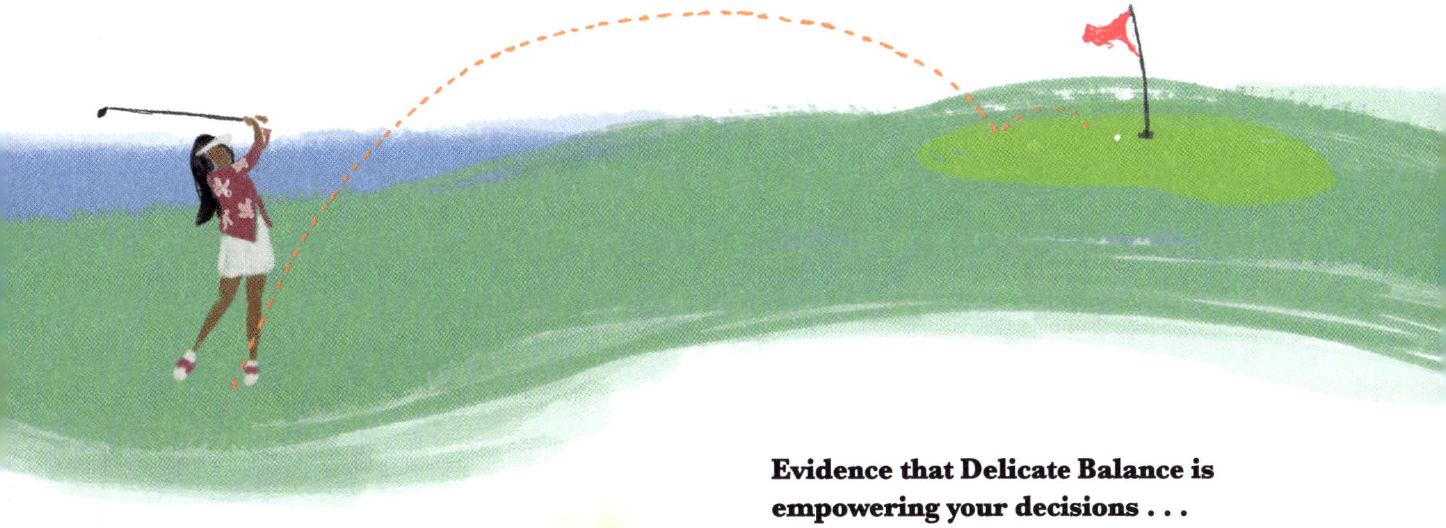

Evidence that Delicate Balance is empowering your decisions . . .

You are more certain about your priorities, with healthy boundaries surrounding them.

You feel happier and more centered.

You remind yourself to be more patient (awareness is progress).

Your goal achievement and personal growth focus on the process and practices instead of the actual specific event.

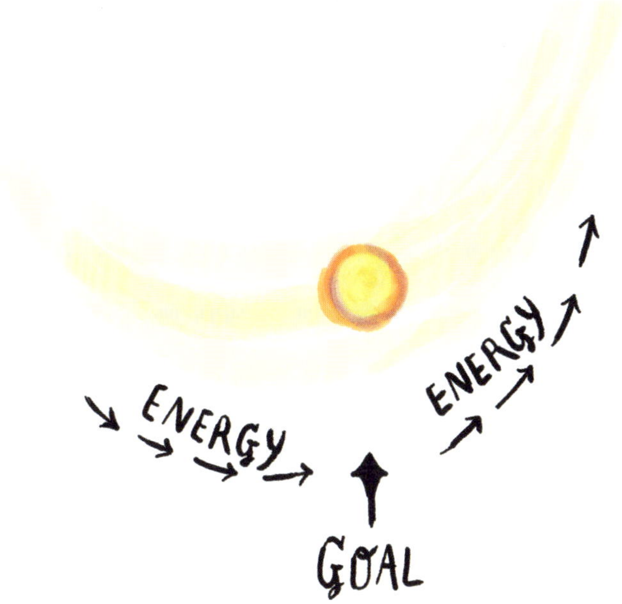

Focus your energy beyond.

When you see signs of the law of attraction working in your life, simply express gratitude, realize that it's a natural part of your improved life experience, and continue your manifestation practices. In other words, begin to expect good things, see good things happening, and enjoy the process without freaking out (because that will stop the good, easy flow).

The Wonderment of Delicate Balance

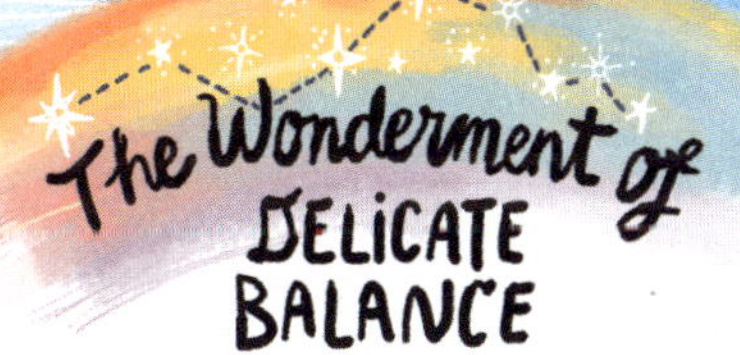

Where in your life do you need to practice Delicate Balance?

Does it require more action or less? Different priorities? More patience?

Take time to feel it in your soul.

As you envision more balance in your life, where do you feel an ease (lessening of tension) in your body? In your head, jaw, upper back, stomach, etc.?

Designing Your Ideal Life

Make eight copies of the worksheet on the next page.

In an ideal lifestyle, how much would you work? Rest? Connect with others? Take care of your health (via exercise, etc.)? Participate in other activities?

Complete your first worksheet by segmenting time based on your ideal life. Label it "Ideal."

Then, complete the other seven worksheets, one for each day of the week. Keep track of your actual activities and time spent on them, documenting as carefully as you can. Label each worksheet "Reality."

Once you have seven full worksheets, compare them to your ideal one. What do you notice between your reality and your ideal?

Are you satisfied with how you are spending your time? Where can you improve?

How realistic is your ideal? How can you adjust your expectations to accommodate the realities of life?

Where can you reorganize your priorities to make your reality more ideal?

24-HOUR WORKSHEET

6 am	**6 pm**
7 am	**7 pm**
8 am	**8 pm**
9 am	**9 pm**
10 am	**10 pm**
11 am	**11 pm**
12 pm	**12 am**
1 pm	**1 am**
2 pm	**2 am**
3 pm	**3 am**
4 pm	**4 am**
5 pm	**5 am**

STAY IN THE FLOW

PRINCIPLE FIVE

HARMONY

There is a coordinated interplay in the Universe, and it is constantly seeking harmony among all the elements within it. Energy is in a constant flow, swirling around in endless currents of vibration.

Harmony teaches us that we experience greater ease and success when we align to the Universe, flowing with its guidance and natural rhythms. In this flow, we experience wonderful synchronicity and wondrous opportunity.

This principle teaches us the wisdom of maintaining Harmony within ourselves to experience harmony in the world around us. When we maintain peace within our souls, we radiate harmonic energy and therefore attract similar energy. When we are in this mindset of equanimity, our decisions are clearer, our lives feel easier, and we are happier.

Harmony means that we remain steadfast to our inner tranquility despite life's ebbs and flows. Therein lies our greatest manifestation strength.

Manifestation Power Requires Inner Harmony

Sometimes, manifestation takes time and repetition. Other times, it happens very quickly. And when our dreams and goals start flowing into our lives, they often happen in a cluster of activity. It's easy to get overwhelmed, but you will learn to flow with it! The principle of Harmony teaches us the importance of maintaining our connection to the Universe despite the topsy-turvy events of our earthly experiences.

Harmony is found where your intentions converge with manifestation. Harmony maintains a steady connection to your priorities by way of your Think/Feel. It is the practice of releasing any conflicting thoughts and emotions that may interrupt the flow.

The principle of Harmony is important to understand and incorporate into your manifestation practice for a variety of reasons.

First, as you begin to experience the intentional manifestation of your goals, it feels exciting. But it also brings change, which can introduce a complex range of emotional reactions based on your learned thought process, history, or circumstances. The principle of Harmony reminds us to stay focused on our authentic intentions above all else. We must stay open to the Universe's inspiration as our source of inner strength and learn to go with the flow of manifestation.

Second, the principle suggests that to manifest swiftly and without limit, we must live in Harmony with others and the world at large. We must seek and maintain consistent positive relationships with all. An overly competitive "us versus them" attitude generates fear and conflict, which are destructive. Because of the mirror-like quality of the Universe, what you wish for others will impact yourself.

Harmony is authentic power.

When your thoughts and emotions align with what you say and the actions you take, you are in your authentic power. You know what's important and what's not, so you are more decisive. Your manifestation vibrations are precise, and the Universe responds with great clarity, too. People interpret this as the energy of authority or success and treat you accordingly.

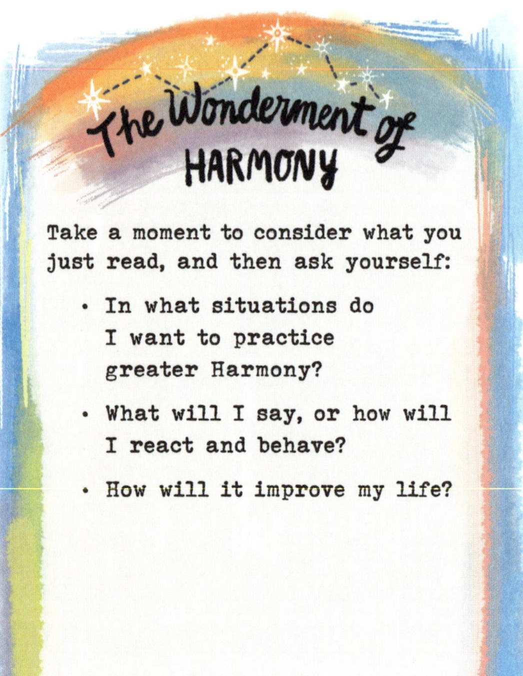

The Wonderment of HARMONY

Take a moment to consider what you just read, and then ask yourself:

- In what situations do I want to practice greater Harmony?
- What will I say, or how will I react and behave?
- How will it improve my life?

Examples

Keep it flowing with practice.

Julia decided that she would finally write the novel that had been dancing around in her mind. With great gusto, she announced her plans to everyone, quit her regular job, and began the writing process. But within a few weeks, she became frustrated with her lack of progress. She fretted about the storyline and forced the words to come out. "I've got to finish this book; it has to be successful. What will my friends think?" she worried.

She continued to struggle with her manuscript as her savings dwindled. After a few difficult months, she abandoned her project and resumed full-time employment. Although humbled, she did not entirely give up her dream.

Upon learning about the principle of Inner Harmony, she realized that applying too much pressure to her goals had blocked her creativity which affected her manifestation process. She learned that when we push too hard, we emit negative energy out of desperation, anxiety, or rigidness, which cannot attract positive results. With this insight, Julia continued her writing project, but this time without eliminating her source of income. Every morning, an hour before work, she would joyfully practice her writing craft, staying in a playful energy. Now, she trusted the Universe, allowing inspiration to flow instead of forcing it.

Eight months later, her book was complete. Julia was overjoyed and proud of herself for achieving her goal. The experience also taught her a valuable lesson in diligence. Practicing regularly, without pressure, allowed her creativity to flow. Not only did she reach her goal of writing a book, but she didn't stop there. She continued her daily practice of joyful writing, and became a better, more well-known author than she ever imagined.

To achieve your greatest potential, rise above the pressure to perform.

Deb was eager to become the top salesperson at her firm, and she was determined to win the year's top sales award.

She consumed all the motivational "go get 'em" videos that she could find. Every day, she revved up her enthusiasm. She boldly chased every lead and obsessively compared her numbers to the rest of the sales team. She agonized over her performance when she started to miss a few sales targets. When some of her current clients began to avoid her, she chased harder. She fretted about her plummeting numbers. As she pushed harder and got more aggressive in her presentations, she struggled even more. Finally, one of her favorite clients told her, "Deb, you are getting too pushy. I don't feel like I can trust you anymore."

This comment crushed her, but Deb was wise enough to take the criticism in stride. She realized that she was applying way too much pressure on herself, her performance, and her clients, and consequently, her goal manifestation was suffering.

After a long, soulful weekend, she rebooted her energy, focusing on Inner Harmony. She released the pressure to compete and compare, and instead shifted her focus back to a more authentic sense of care for her clients.

With a more sincere attitude, Deb regained momentum and began to enjoy her career again. Her new and improved measure of success: To remain in Harmony with the law of attraction and within her purpose of being the best service to her clients.

How to Nurture Harmony Within

Your inside must be aligned to your outside.

Often, in our desire to make things happen, our ego takes center stage. Ego is a human condition that questions our ability to be who we are meant to be, to shine the way that the Universe wants us to, and to attain and enjoy our goals. You know your ego is calling the shots when you feel worry, fear, doubt, or any other emotions that compress, restrict, limit, or dominate, throwing off the harmonic balance of manifestation. To maintain your alignment within the flow of the Universe, filter out the ego's disruptive messages.

As mentioned before, we can pick and choose what thoughts we attach our emotions to. When you become aware of negativity from within, replace it with an improved, more harmonic Think/Feel. With practice, choosing better becomes a natural habit.

Don't give your power to others.

To maintain Harmony, let go of the need to control others! Understand that they are on their own life journey, not yours. Trying to take control of their life is like trying to steer a car you are not driving! Not only is it impossible, but it obliterates your Inner Harmony. Remaining detached from control of others allows you the spiritual space to focus on your journey, while giving others the grace to do the same.

Being overly concerned about the approval of other people is also a disruptive vibration. You cannot control what other people think, so stop giving them the power to distract you from manifesting your most authentic life. When you find yourself worrying about approval, recenter your focus on your connection to the Universe. Allow it to inspire and nudge you back into alignment. This is your life, no one else's. Treat it with your utmost respect and loyalty.

Harmony flows from self-love.

We must maintain harmonic relationships with ourselves. Learning to accept the whole of our beings, flaws and all, keeps our Possibility Puerta open to receiving our dreams and goals. If you desire more Harmony in your life experience, remember to start with yourself. You can't find peace and love in the world if you have conflict or hatred for yourself.

Self-love is not just about feeling good or having confidence. Nor is it self-centered or selfish. It is a key principle for manifestation. When you are peaceful and your priorities are balanced, you can meet others with a centered, whole sense of self. When you treat yourself as a priority, others notice and treat you with greater respect. Consequently, you can advocate better and make wiser decisions, achieving greater personal success for yourself and others.

As your energy swirls in higher vibrations of self-love and Harmony, you attract people who are supportive of you and opportunities that are aligned to your greater good.

To nurture Harmony within, take the time to understand your authentic desires and intentions. The clearer you are about what is important to you, the stronger you will vibrate and the steadier your manifestation energy will be. The way to apply the principle of Harmony is through practice, reminding yourself to align with high vibrations. When a low vibrational thought enters your mind, allow it to go, and replace it with a more harmonic one. Remember the power of your Think/Feel!

Evidence that you are flowing in the principle of Harmony includes . . .

Things that used to trigger you are becoming less bothersome.

People begin to mention that you seem different. And you begin to see them differently, too.

You become uninterested in gossiping about others and much more interested in your own endeavors.

You enjoy the little moments of peace and joy even during busy days.

Goals are important to you, but you are even more interested in the learning and growing taking place within yourself.

You start to challenge yourself by learning a new skill, asking for a promotion, or otherwise reaching for more. It means that you have the power of inner equilibrium to take on new challenges.

Personal Credo for Inner Harmony

A personal credo is a set of guiding principles that influences the way you react, think, and feel. It captures what you consider to be the most important elements of your personal outlook on life. It is very specifically for you, not others.

It is a statement or series of descriptions that keeps you centered, no matter what happens around you. It becomes your reference for inner strength and resolve. It clarifies how to maintain harmonic relationships with yourself, others, and the world at large. A personal credo helps you master your thoughts and feelings. It gives you the power to filter decisions, remain focused on your priorities, and therefore manifest with accuracy.

This worksheet is a start to crafting your personal credo. Through this questionnaire, you can begin to shape your outlook. First, remember these three things:

1. It is your opinion, not others'.
2. Keep it positive; use phrases that feel proactive or nurturing or that advocate for your greater good. Be mindful of your Think/Feel!
3. Identify what you value most about each subject.

Grab a sheet of paper or your journal. Give each of the following questions some thought, and then write a paragraph on each topic. Begin the paragraphs with the words, "I believe . . ."

1. What do you wish to see about the world at large?
2. What are your responsibilities to your community?
3. What does family mean to you?
4. What are the most important attributes of a partner or love relationship?
5. How do you define success?
6. Describe your personal strengths.
7. What will be your legacy?

Now, condense each paragraph into a statement, and transfer the seven statements to the next page.

I BELIEVE

CONSISTENT ACTIONS
ALIGNED TO THE
GREATER GOOD

PRINCIPLE SIX

RIGHT ACTION

The law of attraction is a mirror-like philosophy, and its principle of Right Action states that when we treat others well, we will receive a similar treatment. The quality of your intentions is reciprocated, and so choosing the best for others is also a spiritual investment in your own best interests.

When we establish a strong personal code of conduct that is aligned to what is good and just for the world at large, we are aligned to our own greater good. This includes consideration for others, animals, nature, and the environment. It also includes how we treat ourselves, since we are an integral part of the collective energy.

Right Action, at its core, is the creation and expansion of kindness, for self and for all, as the catalyst for what we desire to manifest. Because what we sow, we will reap.

Staying aligned with dignity and honor will always work toward your greater good.

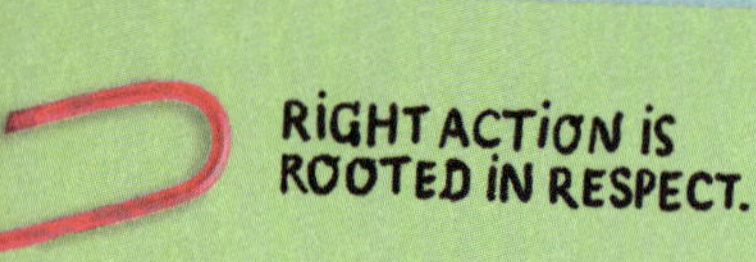

Living Right Keeps It Bright

Right Action is a nuanced, complex principle. It isn't a legal description, or a religious or moralistic doctrine. Instead, Right Action is a more nebulous, personally defined sense of right and wrong.

The discipline of ethics examines aspects of this principle, discerning moral philosophy as it pertains to all aspects of making decisions and life choices. But regarding the law of attraction, there is an energetic cause-and-effect in the reflective nature of how we manifest with this principle.

The way of Right Action involves considering the impact your words, deeds, and intentions will have on everyone and everything involved. It provides a core code of conduct that requires us to think beyond ourselves. It puts us in the mindset of one collective consciousness. We must consider: "The decision I make impacts you and me equally. With this in my heart, what choice do I make?"

Right Action is dependent on a myriad of circumstances. There are some foundational guidelines to determine what Right Action would be, but at the heart of it, Right Action is firmly rooted in respect for others and for self. It honors the independent journey of all concerned, allowing others to make choices for themselves. When our decisions are based in respect and honor, we are more likely to make the right decision; when we allow others to make their own independent decisions, we are honoring their Right Actions, too.

The Wonderment of RIGHT ACTION

Think about the differences between Right Action, the legal system, and religious dogma. How do they individually affect your Think/Feel and, therefore, your manifestation practice?

Examples

The responsibilities of Right Action.

Marcy was the CEO of a successful small business. She loved her job, took great pride in developing her employees, and was an upstanding member of the local business community.

As she celebrated her tenth year in business, a new competitor entered the market. The company had flashy marketing and an intriguing sales pitch. Soon, Marcy noticed that her business was suffering. She examined the competitor's marketing strategies to understand why they were winning and uncovered unethical practices.

Marcy had many sleepless nights over the next year. To compete, she considered implementing similar practices into her sales model, but it would require her salespeople to be dishonest, and she didn't want to risk legal trouble if they were caught lying to customers. She didn't want to dishonor her employee's Right Action. And she was concerned about the damage the bad practices would do to her customers. Yet she worried that if she didn't compete ruthlessly, she wouldn't stay in business, impacting all the employees who relied on it for their livelihood and the community that depended on the service they provided.

Deciding against the profitable yet unethical practices wasn't easy, but she stuck to what she knew was the Right Action. A year later, the competitor was brought up on charges that shut down their business.

Despite the challenging times, Marcy was pleased that she chose the high ground. Her business regained its past momentum, and she enjoyed trusting bonds with her team and customers. And personally, she could walk around her community knowing she had done the right thing for everyone involved.

The easy way isn't the best.

Harold liked to take the easy way out and mastered it by the age of seven. That's when he learned that he didn't have to go to school if he faked a fever by putting the thermometer next to a light bulb. He spent most of his childhood trying to skirt responsibilities. He barely passed high school and went into various jobs, always looking to make a quick buck with the easiest investment of his time and energy. He spent his free time partying with drugs and alcohol, and by age twenty-five, entered the first of many rehab centers.

By thirty-five, Harold had five kids from different women. At the first sign of discomfort, he would pack up and leave without a trace. He spent his life looking over his shoulder, always concerned that he would need to escape a disgruntled lover, employer, or someone else looking for payback.

By forty-five, Harold was burned-out, exhausted with his life choices, and angry that life had been unfair to him. He did not understand the law of attraction's principle of Right Action. His life reflected his authentic (bad) intentions; through a series of misguided decisions, he had accumulated a huge amount of low negative vibrations that could only draw to him similar situations. Life hadn't been unkind; it simply reflected to him what he had put into it.

Teaching kids Right Action may be difficult, but it's much easier than trying to fix a lifetime of bad choices.

How to Know When Your Actions Are Right

Doing the right thing isn't always the easiest or most convenient, yet we intrinsically know what the best thing for all parties is. Or do we?

Here's an example of this conundrum: Is a lie right or wrong? A small untruth might spare someone's feelings (which might be the kindest of all options), or it could hide a wrongdoing (through manipulation and control). The spectrum of right to wrong is truly subjective, so knowing Right Action can be complex.

Right Action is not about looking right or keeping up appearances (that's what our ego tells us), nor is it about blindly following rules without considering how those actions impact our internal principles and Think/Feel. It's about knowing in our soul that we are being the best steward of our life and those we impact. As with everything about the law of attraction, our authentic vibrations are what manifests.

The best way to understand Right Action is to drill down into the cause and effect of your choices.

Ask yourself:

- Will this action harm or help?
- Will it honor all those involved?
- Will it heal a situation or create unnecessary pain?
- Would I want to be treated the way I am treating others?
- Can I empathetically see it from another person's viewpoint? What does it look and feel like?
- Will this create the highest frequency of energy for everyone involved?
- Am I considering the Right Action of others?
- Will this empower others or diminish their power?
- Can I look at myself in the mirror, knowing I took the Right Action?

When you know a better way, correct your course.

As you review your responses to the previous questions, perhaps you are not pleased with your (honest) answers. How can you stop your behavior and begin again, this time by working through the principle of Right Action? Although it can't make up for mistakes in the past, you can always start again, this time doing the right thing.

As Maya Angelou famously stated, "When you know better, do better."

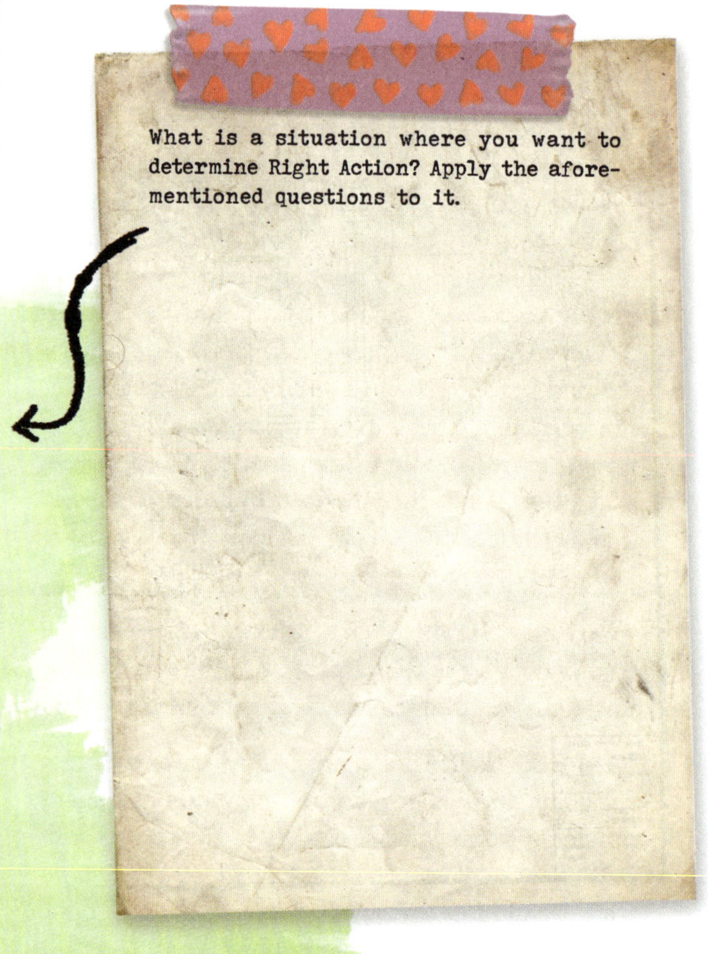

The magical elixir of kindness.

Our thoughts and emotions are choices, as is our outlook on life. What we choose to see is what will expand in our awareness and what we will attract to us. Our words and actions are powerful manifestations of the inner reality we choose to dwell in.

When we extend kindness without expecting anything in return, it's unconditional goodness that we deposit into the collective pool of consciousness. We make the world better, one drop at a time.

But here's the cool thing about kindness: When we extend kindness, we pour it back into ourselves, sending ripples of kindness that reflect the highest vibrations. There is a wonderful, magical reciprocity about the emotion of kindness. As kindness comes up and through our soul, it blesses our inner reserves as well.

When we care for another being, we not only uplift them but also heal parts within ourselves. This is because when we make someone else feel good, it lifts our own emotions. In fact, one of the easiest ways to improve your own mood is to smile at someone else.

When we can see the best in others, it is possible for us to know that we, too, are deserving of love and acceptance. When we can forgive someone else, we are able to see that we can be forgiven. When we believe in another, we hold space for our own potential.

The well of kindness is filled with a magical elixir. When we share it with others, we also benefit from its healing powers.

Evidence that Right Action is working in your life . . .

You are taking more care to analyze the right thing to do, and sometimes, it feels like a struggle. It means that you are more aware of the implications. Doing the right thing isn't always the easiest.

You accept your past without feeling shame or blaming others (when you know better, do better).

You feel completely responsible for your life choices and enjoy the empowerment.

You find ways to provide honest feedback to others without being cruel.

You feel an improved sense of integrity that you are doing the best you can.

What's Your Kind of Kindness?

Deciding how you want to show kindness is part of your Authenticity Thumbprint. Ways of showing kindness can include helping others, making people smile, sharing thoughtful words, or just listening attentively to others so they feel seen and heard, among many other ways.

Brainstorm ways that you want to define your kind of kindness.

You can use a variety of ways, not always the same ones. For example, you can make it a point to smile and greet your new neighbor, or use playful humor to make others smile while in line at the grocery store. Perhaps you make an effort to provide guidance to a new coworker, or find an opportunity to encourage a young child. You can pour kindness into the world by volunteering, mentoring, or creating a positive social media channel.

What are the ways that you enjoy sharing kindness?

Be mindful of how others respond to your overtures of kindness, and experiment with ways that feel most sincere and authentic. And then, add these traits, behaviors, or activities to your Authenticity Thumbprint (from the previous worksheet on pages 45-46).

Consider the importance of kindness—when you've given kindness and when you've received it. Can you remember special moments that have impacted your life?

Allow kindness to heal you.

As you go about spreading kindness, take a moment to be present. Feel your emotions as you watch the other person experiencing your kindness. Oftentimes, they hesitate in surprise, then express appreciation. If they are familiar with your kindness, they may exhibit happy expectation. Feel the goodness of the moment, to connect and share uplifting vibrations with another soul.

As you witness the positive emotions in another person, how does it make you feel? What parts within you does it heal? Uplift? Encourage?

WHAT IS YOUR
RIPPLE EFFECT?

PRINCIPLE SEVEN

UNIVERSAL INFLUENCE

When we consider the magnitude of the entire world, it is easy to think that we are small and insignificant, like a droplet of water compared to the ocean. Yet the ocean is comprised of many droplets of water. It couldn't exist without them. Likewise, our energy vibrations are part of the collective sea of energy that makes up the Universe.

Because we are all connected, our energy outputs create a ripple effect. Our thoughts, actions, and words affect others—not only the people we know, but strangers we pass. We impact the energy of the world with our unique energy imprints, including how we behave, the comments we make online, and even world events that we participate in; they are all part of our ripple effect on the energetic flow of the world and Universe.

Each of us creates a unique energy ripple, influencing the collective consciousness that shapes the reality of the world.

Our Personal Energy Impacts the Universe

When we acknowledge our connection to the Universe, we realize that we affect society every day with our energy. How we choose to use our energy resources represents our respect of and outlook on others, but it also reflects our own view of ourselves.

We all contribute energy that impacts the emotional health of the world. For example, social media provides an instantaneous exchange of energy. With the motion of a finger swipe, we are exposed to posts with pictures, sounds, and messages that affect our Think/Feel, and with our reactions, we deposit energy back into society. Even if we think that our comments and posts are inconsequential or "for entertainment only," we are impacting other users' energy pool, positively or negatively.

Social media also affects our own Think/Feel and vibrational resonance, for better or worse. Where we choose to deposit our energy impacts the world at large and, as we have learned, affects what manifests in our lives.

The way of the law of attraction is one of holistic consequence.

Everything matters! The extreme transparency of the law of attraction requires us to be mindful of our impact everywhere, in all ways.

Every drop of energy builds up goodness or tears it down. We impact the world with every positive or negative vibration. Most of us do so without any awareness of our actions, but if you want to master the law of attraction, then be mindful of what and where you pour your energy into!

Our energetic influence is a loop of action, reaction, and interaction.

Even if we can't fully control what happens around us, we have full control over our Think/Feel. It is empowering to realize that we impact the globe's energy by where we focus our own! When we align our energy with authenticity, we don't need to overthink the process; just stay aware, consistent, and true. Our greater good (and the world's, too) flows from there.

Picking and choosing our preferred focus doesn't mean denying the harsh realities of the world we live in. It means focusing on the things we want more of. It is investing our attention and deliberate energy into what we want to expand in our reality, and when we live through all the principles of the law of attraction, it will be good for the world, too.

Activists can still practice the principles of the law of attraction. Even as we fight for justice or peace, we can maintain a state of emotional balance and purpose (which is vital for our mental health) instead of allowing anger or sadness to consume us. We can remain engaged and concerned with world events without fueling the flames of fear or anger.

By practicing the principles of the law of attraction, we can do good without absorbing the bad energy we want to overthrow.

Examples

Anger leaves a sticky residue on our psyche.

Liza was driving through an unfamiliar part of town. She was headed to an interview for a new position that she was very excited about. She was nervous about presenting herself in the best light possible. As she was trying to navigate the maze of streets to get to her destination, a man in the car behind her pounded on his horn. The blast immediately triggered Liza, and she responded with shouts and a few select cuss words. "You jerk!" she screamed as he swerved around her and raced down the street.

The brief but aggressive exchange with this stranger left Liza in an agitated mood, and as she entered her interview, she was a nervous wreck. Without realizing it, Liza had allowed someone else's apparent road rage to interrupt her inner peace, which disrupted her focus on the task at hand.

What she didn't realize was that man behind her, the one she angrily accused of being a jerk, was racing to the nearby hospital. His son had been injured in a sporting accident. Had she known, she would have been more compassionate—perhaps he wasn't a jerk, just a dad panicked to be with his child.

How often do we assume the worst when we conflict with a less-than-perfect human being and then carry that triggered defensive anger within us, derailing our own Inner Harmony while we send out more negativity? Instead, how can we remember Universal Influence to control our ripple effect?

We may never know our impact on someone else.

On a dreary winter day, I was walking down an almost deserted street. When I got to the intersection, the lights changed, so I had to wait to cross the road. I stood stoically contemplating my dark mood. I thought I was being silent, but my body language must have been telling a story.

An older man walked up beside me, paused, and then said with a friendly smile, "Oh, come on, cheer up. It will be okay; everything will work out fine."

I looked at him in surprise because he had no way of knowing who I was or where I was going. In fact, I was on my way to speak to an attorney and was feeling rather bleak about the situation. However, his comment caught me off guard. I simply smiled or mumbled something, I can't quite remember, but as I proceeded through the crosswalk, my mood lifted ever so slightly. His tiny bit of reassurance comforted me on an emotional level. I realized he was right, everything would be fine, but when I turned around to express my gratitude, he was gone.

I have no way of knowing who he was or why he made the effort to speak to a forlorn woman, but those words were a godsend at a pivotal moment in my life. He will never know what his kind words did for me, but I will never forget.

If we knew how much our comments could mean to someone, even a total stranger, would we try to find more ways to be kind?

How We Can Make the World Better, One Drop at a Time

We are all more powerful than we might think. We are all integral parts of the Universe, and therefore, we all impact its energetic wellness.

Here are a few suggestions for how each of us can improve the resonance of the earth's energy, and because of the reflective nature of the law of attraction, also increase our own positive energy.

- Disconnect from sources of anger or bad energy, whether they are social media, news channels, or individuals who engage in hateful speech.
- Practice filtering your Think/Feel with this question: *Is this thought or emotion going to lead to good or bad energy output?*
- Begin intentionally practicing goodness without expecting anything in return. Random acts of kindness, even simple courtesies, create goodness ripples. For example, hold the door open for the person behind you. Remember, even small exchanges with strangers are depositing good (or bad) energy in the collective pool. Assume the best instead of the worst. Have empathy for others; instead of judging, bestow a loving blessing on them.
- Humor is not funny if it demeans or belittles. It imposes negative energy onto the target, and their emotional reaction reflects and magnifies that negativity. So, edit your humor so that it is mindful of the drops of positivity that you wish to add to (and receive from) the collective energy pool.
- Use your talents, skills, and education to give back and lift up through a charity or mentorship. Donate to worthy causes, especially those that are grassroots and directly impacting those in need. What you give will be magnified with feelings of goodwill via the magical elixir of kindness.

Simple, small practices are worthy investments in the collective consciousness!

Every thought, action, and intention matters. Make yours count for positivity.

The Wonderment of ENERGETIC INFLUENCE

Now that you are aware of your energetic impact on the world, what do you want to change or improve about what you focus on?

You will know Universal Influence is impacting your life when . . .

Your entertainment choices begin to shift. You are becoming aware of the energy attached to them.

You notice the energy when you enter a room or event. You're becoming more sensitive to your surroundings.

You catch yourself silently blessing others, especially those who seem angry, impatient, or upset.

You start to intentionally use your own energy for the betterment of the world.

Your Goodness Ripple

Inside each heart shape, add how you want to positively impact it. What are the practices that you will use to put goodness into each one?

Review the seven principles to answer the following questions. To you, there are no right or wrong answers, except that they need to feel authentic and personal. Keep in mind the manifestation tips and techniques that we learned in Part One to formulate answers that focus on the positive.

- Principle One: Manifestation
  How will I intentionally focus my thoughts and emotions toward success?

- Principle Two: Magnetism
  How will I work on my personal energy to attract success into my life?

- Principle Three: Unwavering Desire
  How will I manage a consistent Think/Feel toward my goals?

- Principle Four: Delicate Balance
  What areas of my life do I need to have more trust in the Universe?

- Principle Five: Harmony
  How will I maintain a centered mindset despite life's ups and downs?

- Principle Six: Right Action
  How does Right Action reflect respect for self and others?

- Principle Seven: Universal Influence
  How will I express kindness to the Universe every day?

WHAT AMAZING EXPERIENCES COULD YOU BE HAVING IF YOU APPROACHED EVERYTHING BY WAY OF WONDERMENT?

Via Wonderment

Great transformations begin with a humble sense of wonder. I encourage you to ask yourself the following:

"I wonder what I can do now that I understand the way of the law of attraction."

"I wonder where I'll be one year from now if I apply the wisdom in my life today."

"I wonder" is an easy, open-minded sentiment with magical implications. When we approach ambitious goals with a sense of wonderment, we create space in our mindset to reach for more than what we would normally consider possible. Wonderment provides a sense of playful curiosity so that we can ease into the unknown without experiencing the pressure of already "knowing" what we are attempting to do. Wonderment opens our minds to finding creative possibilities, making new observations, and considering alternative ways.

By leading with a sense of wonder, we invite the Universe to enter and influence the direction of our lives. That is when wonder-full manifestation can happen, opening the Possibility Puerta and catapulting us to higher frequencies of our authentic potential, blessings, and soul satisfaction.

And now I ponder the wonderment of it all by posing this question: What if you took all the "beliefs" about yourself, your potential and skills, and your past failures and successes and set them aside? With a clean slate, approach everything with curious wonderment.

Then, trust the whispers of your soul that are asking you to honor your truths, your destiny that is patiently waiting to manifest, and your legacy that wishes to be written.

What could you achieve if you used wonderment to release your potential?

Where will you be, who will you be, one year from now?

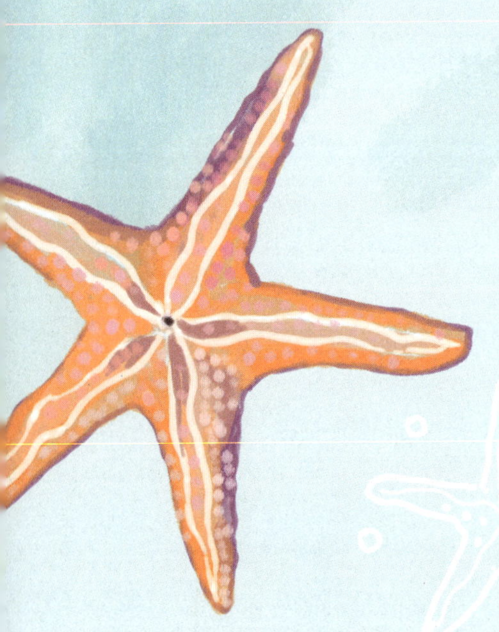

LET YOUR DREAMS
COME OUT TO PLAY
LET THEM DANCE UPON YOUR SOUL.
AND SAIL INTO THE WONDERMENT OF IT ALL!
I am the Master of my Fate.
I am the Captain of my Soul.
~ William Ernest Henley

Acknowledgments

My most sincere gratitude to the following people who helped bring this book to life:

Jennifer and Briana, for cheering me on through the arduous journey of manifesting my creative vision.

Caitlin, Gillian, Lauren, and the rest of the Amplify Publishing team for their enthusiastic support.

Brian, my soulmate, for always encouraging me to shine my light.

About the Author and Artist

KAT GOTTLIEB is a soulful artist, published author, and entrepreneur of several unique, award-winning businesses. She started her career by earning a Bachelor of Fine Arts with an emphasis in marketing communication. Highly creative and insightful, Gottlieb excelled as an independent contractor at an early age, specializing in new business development and marketing, helping organizations and professionals craft powerful brands. She was the founder of a unique, specialty printing and art business that delighted customers around the world. She also cofounded several highly successful businesses in the home improvement industries that innovated cause marketing and other positive, people-centric initiatives.

As an artist and author, she has been published with major brands such as Hay House, Chicken Soup for the Soul, Calypso Cards, and many others. She was honored to receive an award from the New York Stationery Show, and her original artwork has been sold through fine art galleries in the United States and abroad.

Yet her greatest and most impactful experience was raising three children as a single, self-employed mother. It is during this time she developed deep compassion and empathy for those striving to find their own path in life despite society's pressures and demands. And as she courageously crafted her own authenticity, she discovered the wisdom and insights that she shares in her writings and works.

Through her many career endeavors and accomplishments, she has uncovered a passion for the psyche and soul of self-expression and achievement. Now, she uses her creativity to encourage others to live their most authentic expression of life. Kat is an active philanthropist and mental health advocate.

For more art and inspiration, visit KatGottlieb.com

Also by Kat Gottlieb

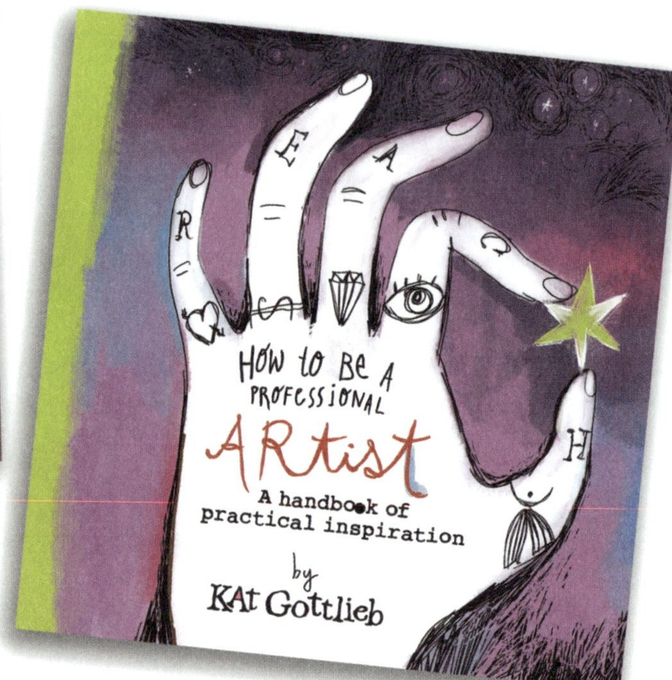

KATGOTTLIEB.COM/COLLECTIONS/BOOKS